The Soul Of Place

RE-IMAGINING LEADERSHIP THROUGH NATURE, ART AND COMMUNITY

MICHAEL JONES

Every place is a journey – and a homecoming.

THE SOUL OF PLACE
IS SUPPORTED BY THE FETZER INSTITUTE

Produced by:

FriesenPress
Suite 300 – 852 Fort Street
Victoria, BC, Canada V8W 1H8

www.friesenpress.com

Distributed to the trade by The Ingram Book Company

TABLE OF CONTENTS

THE SOUL OF PLACE
Michael Jones

*I awake each morning torn between a desire to save the world
and a desire to savour the world. This makes it hard to plan my day.*

– E. B. White

Wherever you stand, be the soul of that place.
Your bright gaze will kindle this old shadow world to
Blaze up once again with the fire of faith.

– Rumi, *One Song*

The Soul of Place *is dedicated to the memory and inspiration of my grandparents, Marion Winter and Ira J. Needles.*

PERMISSIONS

The author gratefully acknowledges permission from the following copyright holders to quote from the works below:

1. Al Purdy. "Beyond Remembering" (partial selection) from *In the Dream of Myself*, Harbour Publishing.

2. Raymond Carver. "The Juggler at Heaven's Gate" (partial selection) from *ALL OF US: THE COLLECTED POEMS*, copyright C. Tess Gallagher, by permission of Alfred A. Knopf, a division of Random House Inc.

PROLOGUE

RE-IMAGINING OUR WORLD: THE PROMISE OF PLACE

I love the earth, and what I see delights me… This harmony has a meaning, these landscapes and these objects, while they are still fixed or possibly enchanted, are almost like a language, as if the absolute would declare itself, if we could only look and listen intently, at the end of our wanderings. And it is here, within this promise, that the place is found.

– Yves Bonnefoy, *The Arriere-Pays (The Back Country)*

This is a book about place and our relationship to it. It is also a book about life and where we find it.

We stand at the threshold of great risk and great possibility. We can step forward and create a home in the future that is alive with generativity and love, or we can step back and risk being consumed by pessimism and fear.

Always when we cross the threshold and enter the deep woods, leaving familiar ground behind, there are feelings both of anticipation and dread — an ancient fear of the unknown — as we enter a new story and leave the old behind.

These transitions have been an intimate aspect of the human journey since the beginning of time. Through the centuries we have evolved from hunter-gatherers to the agricultural age of settlement and stability, to the industrial age and age of technology, to what we may now call the biological age. It is a time of choice as we re-imagine our world no longer as lines and graphs but as circles and spirals in the context of dynamic, complex living systems that are natural, organic and seamlessly interconnected — a world of place.

The biological age is the age of aliveness and promise — a time of discovering a new harmony within ourselves and with life. A time, as writer Yves Bonnefoy describes it, when the landscapes of place may hold within them the key to a deepening experience of enchantment, wisdom and delight.

This idea that there is a soul in places has served as a subtext in my work with leaders regarding the power of place and placemaking. Whether it is artists, architects, community builders and social innovators sharing stories about how a sense of place can sustain us in times of crisis and sudden change, or healthcare leaders searching for ways to deliver integrated services and create communities of care and well-being in times of escalating need, or aboriginal and non-aboriginal leaders exploring ancestral stories of the land and what place is for, or municipalities and rural communities discovering their own cultural story of place, or a manufacturing plant engaging in system-wide dialogues to create neighbourhoods in the workplace, in all these projects one question sounds the heart beat for the rest:

"Where is home, and how do we find our way there?"

Questions of home remind us we simply cope better with the complexities of the world when we feel rooted in a shared sense of place. Knowing where we come from and where we belong helps us feel more grounded and secure. A sense of place naturally calls for us to care for it in some way. In extending this care, we catch a glimpse of a place in the future we seek to create together.

Just as the acorn gives birth to the oak tree, the place we come from holds the code for what we are to become. As such, place orients us, giving us strength for our journey and an optimism for the possibilities the world holds for us as we venture forth.

So, as we enter the biological age, a new guiding story of place is needed, one that speaks to our appetite to inhabit a world that is generous and alive, a world that not only sustains life but also creates it, a world of mutual evocation where we trust that, as we engage with place, place also engages with us, evoking and drawing out something deep within ourselves.

This was the magic of place we held in our imagination when we were young and just beginning to set our course in the world.

English poet William Wordsworth reminds us of that recollected childhood:

> ...at birth, the soul — our life star — rises within us, trailing clouds of glory. For a brief moment we are children of joy. We hear the song of the wood thrush calling us to the dance, we see the meadowland and far hills appareled in a celestial light and feel the world about us alive with the freshness of a dream.
>
> But all too soon shades of adulthood close in upon the dreaming child. We step onto the schoolyard and our deep song — our gift at birth — is suddenly perceived to die away until finally, at childhood's end, it fades into the common light.

Now in darkness lost, our soul travels through the valley of forgetting and sorrow, our exterior a faint shadow of the immensity that lies beneath.

Bound by duty, the soul still remembers a world that is fugitive to its longings now. Yet this desire for reunion burns as an ember deep in the heart, waiting for the wind to kindle it to flame.

These words, adapted from Wordsworth's classic poem *"Intimations of Immortality from Recollections of Early Childhood,"* paint a vivid picture of the soul's longing to experience, once again, the fresh scent of newly cut grass, to feel again the smoothness of a flower petal and, in so doing, be awakened to the brightness of a newborn day.

Too often we take place for granted and don't notice its absence until it is gone. "The loss of soul is painless," philosopher Gabriel Marcel wrote. If there is a crisis of place then, it is a crisis of attention. The recovery of attention will be our primary work as we enter the age in which we will need to shift our focus from analyzing the parts to seeing the complex patterning of the whole. A sense of place educates our senses so that we may reclaim those deeply intuitive dreaming parts of our nature — those aspects we often left behind as we strived to fit into a world that didn't always have room for the fullness of who we were or the gifts we had to give.

Another common theme I heard in these conversations is that the places we create are often placeless because they don't include our stories. It is through our stories we come to understand the kind of affection and inclination we have toward the places that have shaped us and offered meaning and purpose for how we live in the world. In the absence of stories, our sense of place can be designed by others — engineered like lines on a page — rather than imagined as a living presence in our environment, our work and in our personal and public life.

So as we enter the biological age, our ways of coming to know our world will also change. In the industrial age, the intelligence we used was largely based on linear, cognitive or mental abilities. It was a world of parts, objects and things. As we transitioned to the age of technology, we also learned to engage a broad field of human relationships and, with this, a social and emotional intelligence with which to interact. As we enter the biological age, there will be a third shift. We will also develop a new nervous system and with this, a cellular intelligence with which to see beyond our personal identities to the whole vast and marvellous field of creativity including our connection to complex living world. This will enable a way of being that is more porous, transparent and interwoven into the subtle fabric of life itself.

Most importantly, an intelligence based on the life of the cells is regenerative and deeply intuitive. We often don't know how it is that autonomous living cells know when and how and where to move. Nor do we fully understand how it is that the music plays itself, nor how, when there could be nothing, there is something — there is beauty, grace and love. What we do know is that, at the cellular level, we are intimately connected to and aware of the places around us. It is a world where nature, art and community weave together and cooperate harmoniously. Together these will contribute to the formation of a new and vibrant 'creative commons' around which many diverse initiatives may coalesce. It is also a world in which life does not only sustain life but generates new life — a world in which our focus is not only to survive but to grow and thrive in an environment that is constantly regenerating.

So, as we step into a more uncertain future, we will need to place our faith in this deep cellular way of knowing and trust that, even when all else suggests otherwise, life knows what it is doing.

In my own work with leaders, I have noticed how frequently they are responding to this deeper intuition. Many recognize that we are shifting from a world of objective analysis to one of subjective experience — a world in which it will not be the measure of planning and control, but the power of stories and possibility that will shape our places in the future.

This shift is stirring an appetite in many to reconnect with the wilderness not as a retreat from work but as an opportunity to study and learn from nature and living systems and thus understand how the larger ecosystems influence their own life and work. Others seek to engage wholeheartedly with work as a form of art or craft that integrates their minds and hearts with their hands. This includes opportunities to shift from factory models of production to unique creations that are infused with the soul of place and also connect the work of craft and design with opportunities to elevate the beauty of the human spirit in a vastly networked world. And others will find places where they can gather in the commons for conversations that truly matter, conversations that draw strangers together and focus on larger questions about beauty, purpose, meaning and possibility — questions that evoke even larger questions and draw us closer to the central mystery of what it means to be alive.

At first I interpreted these yearnings as a form of nostalgia, a desire to return to Wordsworth's lost innocence of the past. But then I realized that, as we shift to a biological age, we are looking for new ways to become more literate about ourselves and the beauty and aliveness of the human and the more-than-human world that will enable us to fulfill the promise of place in the future.

In service of this adventure, *The Soul of Place* explores different stories of place and placemaking and asks how our collective wisdom of place may provide the underpinnings for what it means to live a place-based life. Reconnecting to this invisible hand of place serves as a daily reminder that the world offers itself always to our imagination. Giving ourselves over to place and placemaking is the inspiration for advancing our progress towards a new promise and the ground from which we can begin creating a more abundant world again.

So, when we ask "Where is home and how do we find our way there?", we are reminded that place is not only a legacy; it is also a prophecy. As such, place is not merely something we return to, but something we grow out from in order to create other and perhaps even better places in the future.

Place is our muse — a presence as committed to illuminating our future as to drawing wisdom from our past.

Of this muse, poet William Stafford wrote, "When you allow me to live with you, every glance at the world around you will be a sort of salvation." (*When I Met My Muse*, 1999.)

And this is the promise of place. It evokes language that connects us to dimensions of human experience that, though often unseen, are deeply felt and healing. When we take her hand, every glance upon our world will be a kind of salvation. Hearing once again our own deep song, the truth of our experience will guide us home.

PART ONE

WEAVING OUR WORLD TOGETHER:

The Three Braids of Place

Where is home? To find it we need a new guiding narrative that accounts for our felt experience of our world — a story that embraces a more sentient, subjective and holistic view of place not as a backdrop but as a life force that permeates everything in our lives. From this perspective, a sense of place offers a unifying story that weaves together our relationship with nature, art and community and inspires us to re-imagine not only how we live and lead but the nature of the universe itself.

BEHIND THE VEIL:

THE RE-ENCHANTMENT OF THE LAND

*This world is indeed a living being endowed with a soul and
intelligence... a single visible living entity containing all
other living entities, which by their nature are all related.*

– Plato

Place happened for me one morning while I performed a short
piano recital for National Park staff and guests in the great room of
the Ahwahnee Hotel in Yosemite National Park. The piano was a
beautiful rosewood Steinway concert grand that had been frequently
played by photographer Ansel Adams almost a century before. It was
late November, a persistent rain was falling outside, and snow was
collecting on the higher peaks, including Half Dome four thousand
feet above us. A lively fire crackled in the stone hearth, throwing
sparks up the chimney. The enchantment of places, and particularly
of wild places, was very much in the minds and hearts of those of us
around the piano.

We had just concluded a senior leaders workshop with the Yosemite
Leadership Academy in the park the previous day. My colleague
and director of the Academy, Pamela Wilhelms, had called the park

administration office a few weeks before to arrange a piano for our sessions that week.

"What do you need a *piano* for?" she was asked.

"It's for the next session of the Academy," she said.

"But why a piano? Isn't this a leadership training session?"

To which my colleague said, "Yes, and in this session we want to explore the park leaders' work in helping visitors discover the power of wild places, how they awaken us to an experience of nature as a dynamic living system — this is what the national parks are for — and music tells this story perhaps even more powerfully than words."

The Yosemite National Park leaders and the Leadership Academy faculty met that week for several days of dialogue on implementing a 21st-century plan for the national park system. One of the purposes of the Second Century Plan was to broaden the diversity of the national narrative embedded in the parks.

This included a renewed focus on "place-based education, leadership and public conversations and collaboration." To explore this issue we engaged in a series of dialogues designed to expand our appreciation for the sacred narrative embedded in Yosemite — a narrative that had been first bestowed on Yosemite and other national parks by revered conservationist and parks steward John Muir.

Our dialogue focused on stories of the power of place and creative placemaking. We reflected on how we have so personalized the natural world that we need to come to wild places like Yosemite to remind ourselves that, while we may strive to expand our own personal achievements, we should not strive to outshine the world. That is, there are spaces and places still that hold within them a mystery and power that exceeds our understanding and invites instead a sense of mystery, reverence and enchantment.

This led us to ask, "What are the stories we need to be telling that bring to greater awareness the life of this place? And what are the stories this place can tell that may shape our own leadership practice?"

We noticed that encouraging participants to tell their stories of place evoked a very different response — a more authentic response — from simply saying, "Tell me something about yourself."

Invitations to tell our stories brought the story teller and story listener into a resonant relationship with the grandeur of Yosemite, which itself is one of North America's greatest natural cathedrals — a home to one of the last wilderness ecologies. Here among these great cliffs, waterfalls and trees, we could feel both vulnerability and resilience among some of nature's oldest and wisest teachers at this threshold between known and unknown worlds.

For leaders in the national park system, the unique environment they steward at Yosemite offers many gifts of place. For example, there is the fondness of and affection for nature's timeless beauty. Furthermore, it introduces opportunities to balance action with stillness and contemplation. Nature's wild places are the last refuge for a deep and profound silence that holds our attention without a purpose or end goal in mind.

Wild places like Yosemite also serve as a portal into experiencing the sense of inclusivity and sacredness of life, of seeing how it reconnects the heart, mind and soul of a community, inviting not only a conversation about our shared past but also contemplation about our future in new ways. And we are taught about our interdependence with a nature-based ecology — one that reconnects us to the spirit or 'genius' — the inner intelligence of a place — which in turn reconnects us to the innate genius within ourselves.

This may be the true enchantment of Yosemite. As one of the last great and original wilderness ecologies, Yosemite offers a mythic experience of the land in its original state. Here we experience the essence of nature and the true spirit of place. While other settings express the essence and elemental dynamics of the natural world, this place is truly unique. Here we experience the uniqueness of our own genius — essential, authentic and complete — reflected back to us.

For leaders in the National Park Service, these conversations of place were transformational. Leaders could foresee an expansion in their roles from being primarily enforcers and rangers, technicians, educators and administrators to taking up the call to be enchanters — to help reveal to others the magic and mystery of wild places.

Heaven and earth, a Celtic saying goes, are only three feet apart. And in 'thin places' like Yosemite, that distance may be even shorter. As one park leader said, "Our work now is to lift the veil and reveal the wizard behind the curtain."

This may be the work for all of us now: to pause, quiet our hearts and find a stillpoint in our own busy lives — to find our own wild places where we may lift the veil in order to discover a more enchanted world. Helping people learn to walk this narrow path between the visible and invisible world is also the leader's new work.

'My Mariposa':

A Mythic Story of Place

A powerful story of place both inspires and sustains us as we make the sometimes-difficult changes that transform our communities over time.

For our community, Mariposa was one of those stories. It was a mythic narrative of homecoming, of the land and of a community and its people. Reliving the story of Mariposa gave us a mythic identity and spoke to the universal longing we each had to be reconnected to our roots, to a sense of belonging and a place of the heart.

Gathering Our Stories

As my community embarks on an ambitious downtown revitalization and waterfront development plan — and also as it struggles to reinvent itself and its identity following the decline of its once-thriving industrial-based economy — community leaders are asking what new story we want to tell. That is, what is the story that speaks to our unique identity and how can this story help us learn from our past in order to create a positive, creative and sustainable future.

In response we have turned our attention to the community's storied connection to the mythical town of Mariposa as detailed by the much-loved Canadian humorist Stephen Leacock

Stephen Leacock was a professor of economics and political science at McGill University in Montreal. During his talks across the world he would often introduce humorous anecdotes of the foibles of life in the small, lakeside community of Orillia, Ontario, close to his summer home on the south shore of Lake Couchiching. He gathered his observations and composites of the townspeople and transported them into the fabled life of Mariposa. His beguiling stories of this stand-in community were eventually published as *Sunshine Sketches of a Little Town.* The stories captured an international audience almost immediately.

Of his creation of Mariposa, Stephen Leacock wrote:

> The inspiration for this book — a land of hope and sunshine where little towns spread their square streets and their trim maple trees beside placid lakes almost within echo of the primeval forest — is large enough. If it fails in its portrayal of the scenes and the country that it depicts, the fault lies rather with an art that is deficient than in an affection that is wanting. (Mainprize, 2012)

Leacock understood how to tap into this deep affection we have for place. He recognized that as we grow into adulthood it is through our connections to place that we keep the dreams of childhood alive. Whether it was the story of the sinking of the paddle wheeler Mariposa Belle — when, after great consternation, passengers discovered they have sunk in only three feet of water and so could call off their rescuers and walk to shore — or the anxieties we all share with one's first banking experience, Mariposa, through the universal language of humour, illuminates how the beauty of the human spirit can be elevated and seen in a more edifying light, our imperfections served up with a twinkling eye instead of the harsh glare of judgment and guilt.

'My Mariposa'

As part of learning and drawing wisdom from these stories, we created a day dedicated to 'My Mariposa.' Our work was to immerse ourselves in the stories of the land, of place and of Mariposa in order to re-imagine a life that could offer a vision of creating a community on a human scale for the future, based on what had worked — or not worked very well — in our past.

Following this inaugural day in experiencing Mariposa, one community leader shared the following reflections:

> Once in a long while we find a sense of place, a place where we feel safe, secure, free to think outside the veil and explore the future of "our place." During the day the doors were wide open, the ball was constantly moving, the stories were unfolding and the inspiration and commitment continued to build. A group of community leaders found the key that unlocked a 'sense of place' and redefined the traditional stories of our community under the overarching mythic story of Mariposa. In the context of these larger-than-life stories, how do we interpret our community? What messages do we want to send to the world? Who represents our stories? What do they mean? Where are the sacred places? And why are our stories important?

These reflections remind us how often we dull our lives, our communities and our landscapes by the utilitarian ways we conceive of them. When we think about our own lives or our community stories in the context of the land, of place and of biographies going back to ancient times, we need to think large. We need to cloak ourselves and our stories in the context of big ideas that include a sense of beauty, mystery and our mythic life together.

The story of Mariposa reminds us that we all come from places and there is a place in each of our hearts for Mariposa. This mythic tale invites us to ask: When have we experienced small miracles, moments when the ordinariness of the everyday is transformed and new extraordinary possibilities are revealed? And what other mythic stories can we uncover that would contribute toward the formation of our own lives, our communities and organizations that may be burnished and brought to life again?

When all is said, we cannot return to the places of our past. As English professor Nick Mount wrote in his review of a recent re-issue of Leacock's *Sunshine Sketches of a Small Town*, "Leacock's stories are specifically about a businessman sitting in his club in the city, a man who left Mariposa as a boy 40 years ago, a man surrounded by other men who have come from other Mariposas and, like him, have forgotten the way home. Yet even if the businessman could find the train back home, 'Nobody would know you now. You have been gone too long. And the city has changed you.'" (Mount, 2013.)

But even as life changes us, we can keep the memories alive. By seeing our land and community not as an abstract engineered concept but as a place charged with hope and personal and collective significance, we can envision a future where our community is revitalized as a destination story and a 'cultural stage' upon which the story of our Mariposa can be lived and told again.

Pathways and Passages:

Walking the Earth in Beauty

Perhaps / The truth depends on a walk around the lake.

— Wallace Stevens

Leacock's story about 'taking the train home' is a powerful metaphor for how places become pathways and destinations. Mariposa, because it was known as a land of kindness and 'good energy,' has been a destination for pilgrimages since the beginning of time. John Muir walked a thousand miles from Indianapolis to the Florida Keys in 1867. Leacock's Mariposa can only really be discovered while walking the streets of Orillia. Canadian author Charlie Wilkins walked from Thunder Bay, Ontario, to New York. To hear Charlie speak of his journey is to share in his own astonishment with how the world opened before him as he moved toward his destination.

Going out into the world is really going in, in order to discover something more of oneself. My previous book, *Artful Leadership*, is based on a series of conversations with a senior leader while taking long lakeside walks in a park near my home. The changing beauty of the wind, the light and the water became our constant companion, a third partner, actively inspiring the themes we explored.

A place is not fully a place until it also becomes a destination. This happens when it tells a story from which everyone can learn. By being wanderers in a place-based world, we recover our own sense of belonging and being rooted to a place larger than ourselves. Being a connector of places helps the visitor discover how to access a community's mythic identity, including its unique local wisdom and traditions through immersion in workshops, festivals, events, stories, its back streets and sacred sites.

Of places and destinations, Robert MacFarlane in his beautiful book, *The Old Ways; A Journey on Foot,* writes that there are two questions we should ask of any strong landscape.

First: "What do I know in this place that I can know nowhere else?" Second: "What does this place know of me that I cannot know of myself?" (MacFarlane, 2012.)

"Paths need walking," MacFarlane writes. Discovering our mythic roots through our experiences of place is often not a static occurrence but a dynamic process of pilgrimage that offers its own opportunities for revitalization and renewal. It is revitalizing because our story is a gift; it is in the nature of all gifts that they stay in motion by being shared with others.

When places become destinations they rely not only on economic drivers but on building destination experiences that are participative and transformational. Some of the common themes of destination experiences include

- Discovering the deeper meaning and spirit of a place.

- Placing an emphasis on co-creating visitor experiences that are engaged and authentic with participative learning in the arts, heritage, culture and the special character of a place.

- Engaging all community members and stakeholders in creating transformative experiences for them and others, such as workshops and seminars, festivals, dramas and tours.

- Creating an ethic and culture of local hospitality.

- Learning to see the extraordinary in the ordinary.

- Building connections, including reaching out to create regional and global conversations with the emerging network of creative destinations.

When we uncover the mythic aspects of place — that is, when we lift up these stories in our imagination in order to perceive their full significance — we also create opportunities for other places to become a source of inspiration and a foundation for revitalization and renewal. This is our legacy: to be full participants in the luminosity of a place-based world.

THE EARTH SINGS:

LISTENING FOR OUR OWN SONG OF PLACE

The structure of nature is also the structure of sound. Both share a symmetry, flow, tone and lyricism — qualities that light up the centres of the brain and unify them.

In the beginning was the word and the word was song. With this song we sung the world into existence. The hills, the trees, the waters, the wood thrush call echoing through the forest at first light, the wind whispering through pine boughs, the waves washing on the shore, the stillness of the night — in every moment the world calls out to our imagination, reminding us that while the mind may wander, our heart knows where we belong. And through our heart we encounter a music in the places of the world that is greater than words can tell.

There is a song within each of us still, and when we hear it we feel full again. Singing comes to us more naturally than speaking, but in our busy world it is difficult to hear our song, and so it recedes in memory. For many it has been lost in time. The great Czech composer Antonin Dvorak reflected on how, in order to hear the earth sing, he would stroll the country lanes, listening for the melodies carried along in the wind like a breath of autumn as the peasants worked in the fields. These haunting themes, born of the deep, rich soil beneath the labourers' feet, inspired his many symphonies and quartets.

For Dvorak these themes came forth like songs from the earth, each expressing the deep promise of the land. But one day the music stopped. The machinery that had been newly introduced into the fields for efficiency replaced the field workers, and the beautiful deep songs that had ignited Dvorak's imagination could not be heard over its incessant drone.

In a place-based world, we are always seeking the inspiration of new beginnings. The artist's ear is like the skin of a drum listening for the deep song. As such, artists serve as the outliers, listening for the subtle connections and patterns of relationship that others do not yet hear or see. Music is one of the purest forms of connection. It marks the passages and turnings in one's life journey. It connects us to the places that illuminate and give meaning to our world.

An editorial in one of Canada's national newspapers, *The Globe and Mail,* reported that the acclaimed Canadian rock band Arcade Fire had, with American director Chris Milk, produced a video that would "stand with Michael Jackson's *Thriller* as one of the greatest innovations in the short history of music videos." (*Globe and Mail,* September 2010.) It was a video production that spoke to how we may travel back through time and discover in our earliest memories how a place has shaped us into who we are today.

Arcade Fire's remarkable video for the song "We Used to Wait" begins with an instruction: "Enter the address of the home where you grew up."

Then the video shows a teenager in a hooded sweatshirt running down an empty, dimly lit street. "It could be any suburban street in North America," the editorial reports. Band founder Win Butler sings, "When the lights cut out, I was left standing in the wilderness downtown." We hear the tale of bicycling through old neighbourhoods, searching in vain for a remembrance of a childhood home amid mazelike, uniform streets.

The video invited its audiences to fill in their vision of place based on their own experiences. In so doing, the band and director had not only created one of the age's video masterpieces, they had also brought into focus how artists connect us to places that help shape us in ways that are often overlooked.

This editorial about music and place brought to mind my own catalogue of music recordings composed over many years. *Morning in Medonte, After the Rain, Touch, Echoes of Childhood* and many others also recounted stories of place, each recording containing themes and melodies inspired by experiences in nature and in the imagination.

Artists are deeply attuned to place and placemaking. It is the source of inspiration that gives depth and meaning to their creations. When I play the piano, I am not alone but rather a part of a larger sentient community — of people, rocks, trees, animals, the wind and light. I am part of everything; there is no distinction.

No matter how jumbled our inner world may be, we can always step into this larger creation and feel nature and experience our hearts lift as we remember what a solace the larger world can be. How, but by the medium of the places in the world, can we find the spark of our own signature in creation? This is what place does.

I also took a special interest in this song by Arcade Fire and its CD *The Suburbs* because it draws upon Win Butler's childhood in Woodlands, the vast corporate suburb of Houston, Texas, where I was a partner with William Isaacs and the MIT Dialogue Project and Dialogos delivering leadership programs at Shell's corporate learning centre for several years. The program, *Dialogue: The Art of Thinking Together,* included an afternoon exploring the participants' personal relationship with place and how it had inspired their leadership practice. From these conversations I discovered that just as place inspires the work of artists, placemaking is also a nourishing concept for leaders in creating environments where others can learn and grow.

At our request, Shell brought a concert grand piano into the centre for this leadership program. Introducing piano interludes into our learning sessions evoked memories among participants about their own feelings and affection for, indeed almost a sacred attachment to, place. These memories included heartwarming stories of how music was a constant presence while growing up in the front-porch culture of west Texas, an experience that defined the soul of place for them.

It is where they enjoyed family and community picnics; it is where they learned to read. It is where they heard stories from their grand-parents — the front porch is where they belonged. It held tremendous sacred significance for them. Interestingly, as facilitators, we were beginning to see how this distinct regional culture attuned them to the dialogue practice we would introduce to them — a practice that brought to the surface their longing to recover the soul of the front porch.

The energy and inspiration that emerged in these sessions caused me to wonder about our current strategies and tactics in leadership development and whether they adequately address the issues and challenges of our day. I had seen how exploring place transformed our leadership sessions, and it made me wonder: would bringing in the power of place and placemaking in leadership theory and practice be a way to revitalize our organizations and communities as well as create ideal conditions for creativity and innovation? It led me to ask these questions:

- What does place have to do with transformative leadership?

- How can our surroundings — place, space and environment — actively work with us as leaders to inspire and revitalize our organizations and communities?

- What do we need to consider and include when creating a future where transformative learning and action can occur?

THE POWERS OF PLACE:

THE BANFF CENTRE FORUM ON CREATIVE PLACEMAKING

The world is our consolation.

– Garrison Keillor

With these leadership questions in mind I convened The Powers of Place forum in May 2010 as a collaboration between the Leadership Development Program at the Banff Centre and the Fetzer-supported Powers of Place Initiative (POPI). The forum was co-convened by Sheryl Erickson, Founder POPI; Renee Levi, Director of Research for POPI; Nick Nissley, Executive Director, Leadership Development; Katrina Donald, Projects Coordinator for Banff Leadership Custom Programs; and myself.

Twenty practitioners from across North America, including social innovators, community builders, entrepreneurs, artists, designers, organizational development practitioners and outdoor educators, came together at the Centre to explore the role of place in trans-formative leadership theory and practice. Core themes we explored included heritage, legacy and the wisdom of places; the philosophy of Indigenous People; the nature of sanctuaries and crucibles; sacred, spiritual and healing places; porch culture; gathering places; third spaces and the commons; community stories of place and creating neighbourhoods in the workplace; the wholeness of places; designing public infrastructure that created a sense of well-being and happiness; displacement and loss of place; the enchantment of wild places; and how art, craft and design related to leadership practice.

The inquiry involved weaving together these diverse themes into three conceptual threads where the powers of place may be found — in nature and ecology, in art, including craftwork and design, and in community and the commons space. To better understand the significance of each thread, we organized our inquiry around our assumptions about place and placemaking, place-based leadership, and our experiences of the power of place.

In the *first* part of our inquiry, we shared and explored several assumptions about place and placemaking we held in common.

- First, that places are alive and speak to us in some way about those things that truly matter in our lives.

- Second, that a language of place is also the language of life. So the language we chose for talking about place may itself bring places alive.

- Third, that art-making in the form of music, story, poetry, movement or the visual arts also helps make place visible and as such is an important form of placemaking.

- Fourth, that all the strands of place and placemaking are inter-related.

- Fifth, that very often we come to know as much about place through its absence as through its presence. So to talk about place is also to explore the experience of the loss of place, of being uprooted or placeless, in a fragmented and broken world.

Thinking as Nature Thinks:

Place as the Fabric of Life

The major problems of the world are the result of the difference between how nature works and the way man thinks.

– Gregory Bateson

In the *second* part of the forum, we shared our thoughts about the leaders' role in place and placemaking for the future. We agreed that we are between stories now. The old leadership story, which was given to us, is no longer adequate, and the new story is not yet here.

In the old story, our leadership has been dominated by machine metaphors from the industrial age and then by technological language from the knowledge age. We have been trained to think as machines think. It is a world dominated by an economically based and quantitatively driven model of leadership constructed around a set of commonly held beliefs.

The first of these beliefs is that our natural instincts and inner knowing cannot be trusted, so we act in deference to the credentials and experience of an external authority. This belief is based on an adherence to an absolute truth that is managed through experts and specialists, policies, external authorities, and standards.

The second belief is based on a notion of separateness and isolation — turning inward to our club or clan and away from the "other." When the other is a threat, we objectify the world, negate the other, and disconnect from nature and the larger world.

The third belief is based on the myth of efficiency and control — that nature cannot be trusted and that everything is up to us. If we don't hold everything together through planning, logic and control, our world will spin out of control.

The fourth is that there is not enough to go around. This belief in scarcity causes us to think that for one to win another must lose. We assume that nature is merely a resource to be used and that the whole must give way to the survival of the parts.

To the extent that our beliefs create our reality, this reality no longer works for us in the ways it may have in the past. We are now beginning to see elements of a new story emerging. No matter at what level we look, whether it is the team, group, organization, community or the larger social field, a new age is appearing. This new story recognizes that places are luminous presences that possess the power to replenish us. As such, these places hold the energy for learning and transformation to occur.

THE TRANSFORMATIVE POTENTIAL OF PLACE

In this new story, we see the transformative potential of place in several ways:

- Our deference to external authority shifts to valuing our own authenticity, including the wisdom to lead from the place within us that includes our gifts and the wisdom of our own inner nature.

- The belief in separation shifts to the search for belonging and an empathic resonance with our world, including an appreciation for our connection to home, to nature, to local wisdom and to who we essentially are.

- The focus on efficiency and control shifts toward a trust in grace and ease, including an appreciation for life's natural unfolding and a willingness to let go and let be.

- The belief in scarcity shifts to an appreciation that, while we may need to work within certain limits, the natural world is based on the principle of abundance and so is replenished, not diminished, by our efforts. Furthermore, when our work is aligned with nature, we not only sustain life, we create life.

In this context, our way of thinking about leadership needs to shift from an industrial mindset in which leaders control from out front to becoming more aligned with the force of nature in which leaders trust what is emergent in the larger field and lead from behind. In a nature-based world, we don't only observe place — we *become* the places we see. Thinking as nature thinks is to also witness the cyclical dynamics of the natural world. Where machines assume a constant cycle of growth, expansion and collapse, nature is always part of a generative cycle of growth, decay, regeneration and new life. Ecologist and poet Wendell Berry writes, "Topsoil is enriched by all things that die and enter into it. It keeps the past, not as history or memory, but as richness, new possibility. Its fertility is always building up out of death into promise." (Berry, 1981.)

Leaders who think as nature thinks are more skilful in shifting our focus to understanding how nature helps us learn from living systems and living processes. Like topsoil, they appreciate that to build fertile ground for a new story they need the richness that comes from the death of old ideas. This also shifts what we want from leaders. It is not that they be warriors/heroes imposing their will in creating a future determined in advance, but that they be thoughtful stewards and gardeners whose artistry involves aligning their work with how nature itself thinks and understanding the generative way the future really unfolds.

This ability to think in new metaphors that are holistic and nature-based was, for us in the Banff forum, one aspect of placemaking. We saw that these leaders emphasize a model of leadership that is more qualitative and ecological in its approach. Thinking together in the context of a language of gifts, seeds and soil-building, we were reminded of terms such as "gathering places," "ecology," "ecosystems," "incubators" and "living processes." Nature is not abstract; it offers us a living language that draws from the 'generative mother' that brings into awareness all that exists. We have been trained over decades to think as machines think. It is time now to learn to think as nature thinks.

One of our forum members, Ed Lambert, a businessman and investor, observed, "Nature-based leadership totally makes sense to me. I would look at the natural environment and say you have soil, you have your seeds, your gifts are in it, you sustain it; you are a good steward."

In the old leadership story, we too often led by role, by script, by credentials and by the advice of experts. It is a world in which we made absolute those qualities of willfulness, busyness and action driven by this sense of fear, control and scarcity. We hunger now for a new sense of balance, one that enables us to inhabit a world that includes those qualities of beauty, trust, stillness and grace that a relationship with place brings.

THE THREE BRAIDS

When the three braids of place are woven together they form an unbreakable bond.

This hunger for a new balance brought us to the *third* focus of our inquiry: the attention we bring to the quality of our environment and the ways we experience the sense of place in the present moment.

The Bow River Valley and the Banff Centre are themselves powerful and sacred places that have held significance for First Peoples for many centuries. The dramatic physical environment signalled to us that we were engaged not only in a conversation but a rite of passage — an initiatory voyage of discovery toward seeing our familiar world with fresh eyes. The circular meeting room's large windows looked out onto the deer and elk that wandered the campus and the snow-capped mountains farther in the distance. This setting deepened our sense of entering into an ancestral journey together.

Our inquiry involved the weaving of a braid made up of three conceptual threads or strands where the powers of place may be found: in nature, art and community. It was also our goal to develop a language through which we could easily cross the threshold from one focus of inquiry to another. In so doing we were creating the opportunity to work at the edges of our respective disciplines and discover not what else we could take from nature but what we could learn from her.

The three-braid concept drew its inspiration from the image of the aboriginal sweet-grass braid, which represents clarity, resilience and strength. That is, when we see place through one lens, it is made more resilient when we see it as interwoven with the other two.

To better understand the significance of each domain of the braid and how the strands were interrelated, we organized this level of the inquiry around several key experiences. Our hope was that, by moving from one focus to another, we could experience how each represented a rite of passage that might reconfigure how we thought about places as we transitioned into and out of them and moved on to the next.

THE NATURAL LANDSCAPES OF PLACE

The way to know a place is not through our minds, but through our feet.

– Julian Norris

To establish the patterns of relationship that help us feel more alive, it helps to begin in nature. Once we have discovered the forms in nature that help us feel more alive, we can go to manmade or organizational forms later on. To describe accurately what we see, we need to revitalize the emotional and sensory content of language. This will give us the expressive power of the words we need.

Our exploration of place in nature involved several hours with Julian Norris, who guides others into the healing force of the natural world.

"Take a walk on the land here and let it speak to you," Julian said. "And say a personal thank-you for the gifts of insight and peace you have taken from here."

"As you walk, close your eyes and let's take a moment to just sink into this place. Love is one of the core aspects of the natural world — and love is the capacity to open up a space in which something else can exist autonomously in relationship to oneself… We are not separate from this place at all; instead we are an integral part with the pine trees, the grizzly bear, the raven and the rock."

Then he invited us to continue walking barefoot in the cool moss among the tall pines high above the waters of Bow River surging over the rocks below. As we did this, he encouraged us to experience a personal relationship with place as a healer, teacher and guide.

I walked slowly, my eyes closed, my senses alert. I realized that the way to opening our hearts is not through the mind but through the feet. The intimate experience of feeling of our feet sink into soft ground is how we come to know the places around us in a new way. I also noticed how rarely we give ourselves the gift of time to allow nature to be not the backdrop but the foreground of our experience.

"We were always here but you did not see us," the spirits said to Faust one day as he struggled to find the meaning of his life. This meaning was to be found not in books, as in the past, but in his own innocence reborn in a firsthand visceral experience of the natural world.

To reacquaint ourselves with this world, we would need to take more time to walk barefoot on the cool moss and listen again for the language of the wind rustling the pine bows.

The Artful Landscapes of Place

I don't care what shape the finished building or its details are – provided only that they are natural.

– Christopher Alexander

Our exploration of place in art involved a walkabout of the Banff Centre campus in order to get a sense of the built environment and its overall surroundings, paying particular attention to the subtle qualities of what was around us.

We were asked to locate something — the shape of a doorway, window, arch, courtyard, plant arrangement — anything that gave us the idea there was something alive and vital there. We were to notice the thoughtfulness and attention behind the design and how this in turn created an atmosphere that felt right and natural and explore together what that *something* was.

We did this by wandering around, noticing places that felt inviting and welcoming and those that didn't. In this way, we were able to get a sense of the Banff campus and its overall setting. We did this slowly, paying particular attention to how we might generate a language of place through sight, sound, touch, taste and smell.

Guided by the work of architect Christopher Alexander in his groundbreaking book, *The Timeless Way of Building*, we then asked ourselves such questions as "What exactly is this 'something' that feels alive? What is it that enables a space to feel welcoming and hospitable? How is this space designed and crafted, and what is it in the relationship between the elements or forces that contribute to this something feeling good?"

In taking the time in silence to notice our surroundings and ask these questions, we were trying to capture the essence of the environment and its aspects that led to us feeling more vital and alive. We observed that, to truly see a place and appreciate how it actually is, it was important to let go of our opinions regarding how places ought to look.

One factor that contributed to the transformative setting of our meeting space was including the design aspects of craft embedded in various expressions of art. Philosopher Blaise Pascal once wrote,

"The most unhappiness comes from not being able to sit quietly in a room." To enter and sustain this quiet space together, we tapped into the regenerative force of place in many ways, including stories, poetry, art and music, each crafted as a reflection of the spirit of the moment. By being deeply immersed in the Banff environment, which was dedicated to the expression of art in all its forms, we discovered diverse expressions of beauty. This enabled us to practise the language of placemaking and move in an appreciative way with the ebbs and flows and patterns of what was emerging, rather than resist or move against them in some way.

THE CULTURAL LANDSCAPES OF PLACE

All stories of place are healing stories.

Our search for community involved sharing the gifts we experienced and appreciated in each other — a way of being together that has served as the foundation for building cultures of gift consciousness in economies and communities throughout time.

Seeing the gift in the other is a healing act. It is an acknowledgement that place itself is a gift offered gratuitously; by living in our gift, we find a way of giving back. Yet many leaders don't know their gifts, and when we don't know or acknowledge the gifts in ourselves that we hold in common it is more difficult to see them in others. By taking this time to fully take in the other, we not only named their inner strengths, we also developed a language of appreciation that enabled us to articulate the gifts we saw with greater ease and precision.

In this process we discovered that gift cultures are also place-based. Placemaking helps us see; we are given the gift of sight. As well, gift cultures are place-based because the seeds of our own innate potential need fertile ground in order to take root and grow.

We also noticed that, when we typically thought about our own gifts, they were based on things we *did* — our accomplishments, goals, projects, outcomes and results — not on who we were. But, here the gifts others saw in us were based on inner qualities of being — qualities closer to our true nature that others appreciated in us.

It was much easier to give this kind of affirmation than it was to receive it. We can control what we give but not what we receive. This experience was nurturing and full of surprises as we learned that it is the community that calls out the gift in each of us and that others see this gift and how it serves the community more clearly than we may see it in ourselves.

A World Too Full
to Talk About:

Creating Living Webs of Connection

Out beyond ideas of wrongdoing
and right doing there is a field.
I'll meet you there.
When the soul lies down in the grass
The world is too full to talk about.

– Rumi

As we wove together the three strands of the braids of place we also noticed we were developing new habits of mind and new social fields for placemaking. These understandings seemed to be beyond words and emerged in the resonant field we had created among ourselves and that suggested new ways of feeling, knowing and being together.

- Through our relationship with place, we were learning to see our world more comprehensively and less selectively.

- Places were teaching us how to feel our world more deeply before we took action to change it. Places also enabled us to recognize patterns and connections rather than seeing things in isolation.

- When we saw our world through the lens of place, we also expanded our notions of what is real, stretching our awareness beyond the verbal-intellectual to include other sources of knowing, including intuition, sensing, feeling and touching.

Together these habits of mind represented alternative ways for engaging in and experiencing our world that are mostly invisible to the rational mind.

It was working along this threshold of making the invisible visible that was key to our work. Too often, when the rational mindset is dominant, nature becomes a resource, art serves as a distraction and community members become consumers rather than citizens.

These habits of mind were helpful in better understanding how we could bring this work back to our communities and organizations. It meant we became more deliberate in creating a learning space together that made the experience of placemaking both visible and possible.

For example, to ensure we had solid ground underfoot, the setting and the structure of the conversations became particularly important. This included the tone setting of my own piano music, which created a listening field for hearing the words of others more clearly. This was augmented through the introduction of poetry and stories, the gentle and welcoming facilitation, and the fresh thinking we shared. This shifted our learning container from a formal classroom environment, where someone was teaching from up front, to something more like a campfire retreat.

As a campfire retreat, it felt as if we were *inhabiting* our learning space rather than *observing* it. And when we experience inhabiting the space, our primary concern is to care for it — to allow it to be hospitable and welcoming rather than trying to over-organize or structure the space in some way. This did not mean the space was disorganized — rather, the spirit of the design arose more from an inner coherence that was both elegant and prescient in some way. The space itself seemed to anticipate our needs and our moves in advance of our more focused and intentional minds.

As a result, our leadership became even more broadly shared. We took our cues from the group regarding how we might best engage and inquire into the three braids of place we wished to explore.

We also reflected on how our gifts are uniquely fitted to a place and how the place itself can serve as an incubator for transforming our gifts into creative work.

Examples of creative artists and the places that have made them who they are include Robert Frost and the apple orchards of New Hampshire; Henry David Thoreau and the rolling fields and woodlots around Concord, Massachusetts; Emily Dickinson and the formal atmosphere of the small college town of Amherst, Massachusetts; Willa Cather of Red Cloud, Nebraska, who wrote of the high plains and grasslands of the early American heartland; and poet and pediatrician William Carlos Williams and his connection to the modest industrial lands around Rutherford, New Jersey.

Serving the
Well-being of the Whole:

Place, Culture and Character

Place is the wellspring from which all life flows.

Leaders, like poets, also come from places — and make places for themselves — that instill and reflect certain deep values they hold regarding who they are and how they lead. Being place-based helps leaders discover what 'uncommon' actions they can take in order to be unique and comfortable within their own skin. A sense of place also teaches them how to create places for others in the form of cultures, relationships and environments — and an atmosphere — which will enable others to do their best work.

For Paul Polman, chief executive officer of consumer-products giant Unilever NV, to be place-based is to treat thousands of small tea farmers with the same regard as he does shareholders. To him, serving the common good in business always served as the incubator for creating a positive future.

"When our generation grew up after the Second World War, our parents wanted the same kind of thing; they wanted us to go to university and have a better life. Most of them were working for the greater good of society," he said in a March 2013 *Globe and Mail* interview.

Soon after the height of the 2008 financial crisis, he realized the company had become too internally focused. In their efforts to meet shareholder value, Unilever had lost sense of who they were and what they stood for. Polman also realized this was an ideal time to kickstart change. He and his executive team decided to get the company back to its roots by re-engaging their own mythic story of place.

> I went back into the origins of Unilever, to discover that [founder] Lord [William] Lever invented the bar soap in Victorian Britain because cholera was such a problem. One of two babies did not make it beyond year one. The problem he tried to solve involved hygiene. In the origins of many companies, people were working in the interests of society, not in the interests of shareholders alone. Focusing only on shareholder value is a very destructive concept. (Ibid, 2013.)

In order to create a culture of place, Polman believed, the business environment needed to be something other than a 'personal wealth accumulator.' Instead he was committed to bringing the world back into balance through encouraging leaders to serve the greater good and put this ahead of their own self-interest.

Paul Polman's quest to redefine the purpose of business in the context of the mythic roots of placemaking is echoed in another example. For the past six years I have been a part of a faculty team offering a four-week creative-leadership program for senior executives in a third-generation, Texas-based construction-engineering company. The founder, H. B. Zachry, in his own statement of character entitled "I do not choose to be a common man...", talks about the essence of who he is:

> I want to dream and to build, to fail and to succeed
> — never to be numbered among those weak and timid

souls who have known neither victory nor defeat....
Yes, I want to live dangerously, plan my procedures on
the basis of calculated risks, to resolve the problems of
everyday living into a measure of inner peace.

It was the heartfelt expression — and the defining myth — of a
founder and leader of a global company and an independent and
resourceful leader, someone dedicated to the well-being of his
employees and who had himself been shaped by the hard-scrabble
demands of the land he had grown up on.

Like seeds to soil, each is fitted to the other. In every instance for
such leaders, place came alive through their leadership, just as their
creativity came alive in the presence of the places they both cared for
or came from.

In a similar way in our Banff forum, we did not hold a fixed idea
of what the processes meant or had to be, so we were able to take
risks that reflected the strong forces that had shaped this dramatic
mountain environment. By letting the visceral elements of the place
influence and inspire us, we were able to achieve even greater fluidity and resonance.

Perhaps this is also true of place and placemaking: the place itself is
not static but in a state of constant evolution or mutation. Where
there seems to be nothing, there is always something. And this
something represents the unifying force of place, deep and mysterious — the 'topsoil' from which all life springs and to which it
eventually returns.

The Soul of Place takes the seminal ideas generated in the Banff
forum and develops them to better understand the nature, dynamics and practices of place and placemaking. This understanding is
central for leaders who wish to tap into the transformative power of
place and prepare for the creative age to come. In this context, *The
Soul of Place* will explore the importance of the following ideas:

1. Appreciating the need for a shift from an economic to a more place-based and ecologically minded worldview.

2. Understanding how a greater awareness of place contributes to re-imagining leadership, community and organization.

3. Constructing a language of place that can contribute to the work of transformational learning and change.

4. Exploring frameworks of place more broadly through the lens of nature and ecology, craft and design, and community, celebration and the commons space.

5. Discovering how our own mythic narrative is enlivened and takes on greater meaning when expressed through the perspective of place and placemaking.

6. Exploring levels of learning and communications — tactical, strategic and generative — and which levels are specifically place-sensitive.

7. Exploring the role of art (music, poetry, conversation, stillness and story) in place-based transformational work.

8. Offering a map for engaging in creative placemaking and creating cultures of place as a foundation for regenerative learning and change.

PART TWO

THINKING AS NATURE THINKS:

The Natural Landscapes of Place

We are between stories now. We are evolving from the world dominated by technology and entering the age of biology when there will
be a resurgence of interest in learning how to work with the forces
of nature rather than against them. It will be a time for following
what feels most natural, organic and heartfelt. And it is a time for
understanding that we do not enter the world; we grow out of it.
The seeds of our own unfolding future lie deep within ourselves.

An Ecology of Hope:

Creating Healing Environments for Belonging and Well-being

We evolved as creatures knitted into the fabric of nature, and without its intimate truths, we can find ourselves unravelling.

— Diane Ackerman

In Ecuador and Bolivia, exploring new paths toward growth that is attuned to living well is called *sumak kawsay*. It's an indigenous concept that means developing in harmony with nature. By attempting to marry economy with ecology, they have written into their constitution the recognition that nature, including trees, animals, and rivers — entire ecosystems — have the constitutional right to exist and flourish as full members of the human and more-than-human world.

How do we bring this practice of living well and nourishing the natural world to the leadership of our own communities and organizations? And how do we transform communities into healing places that can nurture a sense of belonging and well-being?

One of my first experiences talking to community leaders about the power of place was at a regional conference exploring a more holistic and transparent way to measure societal progress.

It was an opportunity to bring together local leaders in health, culture and public administration to look beyond economic indicators such as GNP and take into account the full ecology of a community's assets. These include its local distinctiveness, unique story, the gifts of its natural surroundings and its aspirations and dreams for a positive future. We could then explore how these assets could contribute to living well, using indicators for happiness and belonging — measures that could track our progress in increasing our communities' sense of health and well-being.

To facilitate this conversation, we deliberately created a sense of place — as we had at the Banff forum — by weaving together music, art, time in nature, storytelling, guided dialogue, small-table group conversations, and personal reflection. We hoped it would feel natural to share questions and reflections, enabling participants to come into the moment, listen and speak from the heart, and connect with the stories that mattered most to them and their communities.

At the heart of these conversations was the opportunity to imagine and reflect on questions that could influence the quality of their well-being now and into the future. We asked questions like these:

- What are the places and spaces in your community where you experience the greatest sense of aliveness, vitality and significance?

- What are your stories of place, and how do these stories bring to life the collective memory of your community?

- When you think about the future relationship of your built environment, the health of your population and community well-being, what really matters? That is, what are the hopes and dreams you hold for the community, and what story do you want to create for the future?

- To build the ground for your future, what do you want to conserve and what needs to change? What are your current challenges, dilemmas, resources and gifts?

- What new story is possible by creating a culture of possibility in your community, and what kind of leadership will be needed to bring this story into being?

We framed these questions with the expectation that a language of place would build social capital. That is, it would give leaders the tools to embrace uncertainty and speak imaginatively about what is often difficult to express. It would also help them appreciate that, to create livable communities, they needed to think not only as engineers and economists but also as social architects, ecologists, artists and placemakers who could take the context of the bigger picture and lead adaptively, unbound by a narrowly structured script or plan.

With this in mind, we knew we needed to begin with stories of place. Through these stories, by naming the distinctiveness and what is 'uncommon' in each neighbourhood and community, we would be able to resist the pressures of convention and uniformity.

WISDOM SITS IN PLACES:

MEETING IN THE LAND BETWEEN

During the first evening of the Banff Centre forum, Brian Calliou, director of Aboriginal Leadership Programs, invited us to meet around a fire in a large tepee. He shared the story of his people and the traditions in the Bow River Valley. He spoke about how his people, the Western Cree, had for over ten thousand years found medicine in the Bow Valley. He reminded us that, when a people have practiced the art of longevity with an extended presence on the land, places take on greater meaning. This significance grows as the shared history of the community's memories of time and space are expressed through their songs and stories.

Furthermore, while the Europeans desired to master nature through recreating and re-arranging it to meet their needs, First Peoples used their ingenuity for place in other ways. They accommodated themselves to their surroundings and related to it with an inherent caution and respect. Unlike the Western mind that considered nature as inexhaustible and took from it without regard, First Peoples took as little as met their needs.

Often the Western mind's indifference to place leads to overlooking the significance of places for others, places that others consider animate and alive. As writer Barry Lopez points out, for some people a sense of place does not end at the surface of their skin. Their senses extend outward to include the landscape. When the land is disfigured or altered in some fundamental way, it literally causes physical pain; their psychic and emotional body is being affected as well.

When we are deaf to other people's places and stories, we may not be able to hear our own. So, in placemaking, it is important to reconnect with the kind of ethic that grows out of the wisdom that others gain from their intimate connection to place and story, with nature and knowing what the land is for.

Since this regional learning conference on community belonging and well-being was being held on the land of the Chippewa First Nations, we invited Sherry Lawson, a highly regarded local native writer and storyteller, to be our opening speaker.

In speaking of her relationship to the land, Sherry talked about how the elders of the community served as the memory-keepers of place. She explained how, in the narrative of the land and people, every place is a meeting place.

"You are on sacred ground," she reminded us. "When you are on Indian land, you need to learn together in Indian ways." She told us how their community story is woven into the fabric of the land and sustained in the mythic story of Mnjikaning.

For over 4,500 years, the story of Mnjikaning has been the unifying narrative connecting the diversity of tribes and cultures of all peoples. Mnjikaning means "gathering together," and for millennia many gathered there from all directions to draw nourishment and strength from the fish that were found in the clear waters. But it was not only the fish that made this the destination for so many. It was the creative energy of the land and the hospitality of the people who made their home in that place. They were the "keepers of the fish fence." The weirs, as they were also known, are still located in The Narrows, a small channel that links two large lakes: Lake Simcoe, a deep, windswept lake to the south, and Lake Couchiching, a narrow, long, shallow winding finger lake to the north. (Couchiching in Chippewa translates into "Lake of Many Winds.") The Narrows was just a mile or so down the shore from the site of our meeting.

The Chippewa Nation had a large settlement here and developed the weirs as an innovative method of trapping fish. This was how it became known as a sacred location for the annual gatherings that brought together First Nations from across what is now northeastern Canada and the eastern United States.

It is where they met and shared their home with some of the first European settlers. Over the centuries, the "story of meetings among the many" was not only a bridge that united the diversity of tribes and cultures, it also animated their environment — retold time and again in the soil, the wind, the water, the light and the sky.

In addition to being a place of healing and nourishment, this land between was a powerful and symbolic metaphor for a meeting place that marked the edge of the limestone plain and the warm, shallow pickerel lakes to the south and the deep granite and cold trout lakes of the pre-Cambrian shield to the north. To the south were mosquitoes and strawberries; to the north, blueberries and black flies. The people of Mnjikaning were unique in that they lived simultaneously in two worlds — a "land in the middle" — where they were required to be masters of two distinct biospheres, each with its own complex ecology of fish, fauna, vegetation and animal life. (1)

This notion of being stewards of the land between became one of my first lessons about place. The land between serves as an *ecotone* — a unique transition zone between two biomes. It is an area between two adjacent but different biospheres, specialties, practices or communities. The word ecotone itself is a combination of *eco (logy)* plus *-tone,* from the Greek *tonus* or tension (Van der Ryn, Cohen, 2007). In other words, places where ecologies are *held in tension.*

Ecotones are points of contrast between two vibrational fields resonating to different pitches or tonalities. It is in the presence of one that we come to better understand the other. In music, it is the contrast between major and minor keys. In nature, it is the temperature layers in lakes, the shorelines and the spaces between forest and meadow.

These are high-nutrient zones where fish and animals come to feed. An ecotone may appear as a gradual blending of two communities across a broad area or manifest as a sharp boundary line. However it appears, an ecotone represents a rich field of diversity for intense creative engagement; it is at the intersections or edges where the richest exchanges and interactions take place.

When Sherry began her story of living in the in-between space, everyone listened attentively. For a moment, the cell phones were silent, and everyone was focused on her words. The veneer of our day-to-day identities dropped away. We were no longer students, nurses, politicians or accountants.

Later, as we shared our own stories of place — stories unrehearsed and, for some, offered for the first time — words seemed to form on our tongues as we spoke, and our way of seeing our world was transformed. We were tapping into those deep, core mythic energies — of healers, warriors, magicians, enchanters, weavers, shamans and visionaries — ancient identities that have defined our role in a place-based world for thousands of years. In stepping across this threshold and outside the norm, we had taken up the thread of our ancestral past and assumed our natural place on the land, one that had been long forgotten and needed to be remembered again.

With her opening words, Sherry welcomed the community and invited us to retrace with her one small part of the 5,000-year-old story that had been her people's journey of place and placemaking. To bring home this experience, we stepped outside for an early-afternoon walkabout to find a place that spoke to us, much as Sherry had referred to how her grandmother's gravestone had spoken to her. Whatever it was — a tree or a bush or an open grassy area by the water — the purpose was to engage with this ancient story of meeting by sitting with our own question and letting this place speak to us about new possibilities. As we were warmed by the fresh breezes of Lake Couchiching that unseasonably warm November afternoon, we re-experienced the perennial story of place.

This practice of letting places speak to us links to both contemporary and ancestral wisdom traditions. In *Wisdom Sits in Places,* Keith Basso, an anthropologist from the University of New Mexico, writes of his work with the Western Apache in Fort Cibecue, Arizona:

> A people's sense of place, their sense of their tribal past, and their vibrant sense of themselves are inseparably intertwined. It is only in reference to place and to the earth that their identity can survive. Therefore, knowledge of places is closely linked to knowledge of the self, to grasping one's position in the larger scheme of things including one's own community, and to securing a confident sense of who one is as a person. (Basso, 1996.)

WORLDS IN TRANSITION:

WEAVING TOGETHER ANCIENT WISDOM
WITH MODERN THOUGHT

*In any biotic field, life exists not only for our
consumption but for our enchantment.*

— Aldo Leopold

By bringing together old ways of knowing with new pathways to
innovation, we were creating opportunities to re-enchant a disen-
chanted world. Much of placemaking involves exploring these places
of transition between two or more worldviews or ecosystems.

For the communities that make up the regions of North Simcoe–
Muskoka, the meeting to launch the Community Index for Well-
Being on the shores of the Lake of Many Winds was an invitation
to expand their own sense of self and see their place in the natural
order of things by listening to Mnjikaning's timeless story of place.

This conference was not only an exercise in talking together; it was
symbolic of a larger ritual of meeting. It was a reminder and an invitation to be together in a way that could serve as a foundation for
meetings in the future.

In the bigger picture, these conversations about place also served as a reminder that the answers to the major challenges in the future will not only be economic or technical but nature-based and ecological. How do we navigate the nexus across these diverse worldviews.

In the aboriginal worldview, preserving, protecting and being a good steward of the land takes priority over extracting and exhausting its resources. And spirituality, ceremony and mutual respect are more valued than competition, material possessions and 'succeeding.' They see place, and the individual, in the context of a circle of sacred relationships and feel at home in the human and more-than-human world. Western civilizations tend to see the individual as separate and above nature and view place from a more linear-thinking pragmatic worldview.

According to ecologist Aldo Leopold, author of the classic book of land stewardship *The Sand County Almanac*, "This more linear or economic worldview holds that in any biotic community, most members of the natural community, from songbirds to wildflowers, have no direct economic value. Less than five percent may be sold, harvested, eaten, or put to economic use in other ways. But the ecologically minded understand that the value of the five percent is wholly dependent on the stability, integrity, and health of the other ninety five percent." (Leopold, 1999.)

Leopold's observations echoed our dialogues on place and place-making at Yosemite and Banff. That is, to master the art of living well, life must exist not only for our consumption but also for our enchantment. This enchantment is not superfluous. Because it encourages us to be good stewards of place, it ensures the existence and viability of the small part that does offer economic benefits.

While we may define ourselves as rational and analytic, we cannot overlook the aspect of our own nature that finds its well-being in our passionate search for pleasure and in our experience of the beauty and harmony of our world. We are, at our core, sensuous beings who simply live better with more rather than less nature. Nature teaches us to grow while looking. Nature, as a partner in creation, is not mute. It is speaking to us all the time; we just have to listen.

As we learn to re-engage processes that serve to enrich the ecology of the community and create economic success in the long term, we need to see our human systems not as linear and causative in a conventional way but instead as organic and integrative. Nature is leaderless. The re-enchantment of our world begins with seeing it as a living, self-governing ecosphere wherein many complex and interrelated patterns and factors are self-organizing and constantly at play. As such, these patterns are also a reflection of our own inner landscapes of place.

It is toward this more personal exploration of place that I would like to turn next.

PLACE AS A TOUCHSTONE:

BEING 'AT HOME' WITHIN OURSELVES

To recognize the quality and principles of a place and the changeless principles behind it requires a corresponding quality within oneself – a place that knows, a touchstone that everything can be measured and understood in relationship to.

– Kinkead Martine

Any exploration of the soul of place begins with this conversation with ourselves: What place have we come from, and how has that place inspired and affected who we are now? How is our interior landscape a reflection of the character and subtlety of our exterior world?

These days, much of our world seems lifeless and bland, devoid of the arresting beauty that may have been more visible to us in times past. When everything around us begins to look the same, it is difficult to find places that speak to us and satisfy our hunger to connect with the touchstone — the divinity of place — we hold within ourselves.

To begin this journey, we need to take notice of those cracks or openings in our experience — those moments when there is a break in our routine, and our attention and the feeling of connection with the place around us is suddenly ignited. This sudden sensation of 'at-homeness' connects us to the unique and exquisite trajectory of how places weave their way into our work and life. This is the promise of place, an invitation to come into an alignment and harmony with our own inner nature. In the presence of place, we feel more alive, present, rooted, and native to ourselves. We feel more at home with those elusive qualities of authenticity, creativity and spontaneity — qualities we most value in ourselves but that are sometimes difficult to achieve.

While we often see artists and poets as those who have a particular receptivity to letting places speak to them, it is available to anyone. It requires simply being open to the nuances of felt experience through our direct encounters with nature, art and community. In those moments, we are able to set free our imagination from the literal influences of our analytic thinking and abstract thought.

Whether we are fortunate to have come from a beautiful, inspiring place or not, we all come from somewhere. And while the beauty may be less obvious, there may be an aspect of the place that can engender a strong sense of connection. Others who find no such inspiration in their original homeland may find other places that speak to them in their life.

After a few moments of listening to music at the Banff Centre's Powers of Place forum, we looked at the place we came from and how it inspired who we are as the basis for an 'ecoduction.' Ecoductions serve as a way of introducing ourselves based not on what we do for a living, who our family is or how we spend our leisure time, but on where we come from and how this sense of place inspires who we are, how we are and what we wish to become.

Our early and sometimes-profound experiences of place shape who we are today. This ecology of our early development is just as telling (perhaps even more so) of who we truly are as our social constructs. These conversations of place often include the physical environments of our childhood, the natural geography we were raised with and the beauty of the land that reflected our first intimate encounter with our world.

By asking "What is the place you come from?" we are invited to explore how our shared love of place serves as a unifying force for discovering a common ground. It helps us appreciate how place weaves its way into our personal landscapes, real or imagined, and serves as a touchstone for how the natural world speaks to us. Most important, it invites us into a conversation with ourselves that is as immediate as it is illuminating. As one participant observed, "I don't know the people I work with as intimately as some of the people here whose stories we have shared in these past few moments."

This observation reminds us that place matters perhaps more than we know. Conversations of place serve as a conduit through which the most personal and deepest aspects of our experience are also the most universal. This may help us understand how it was that those early cultures that were most integrative and cohesive also built the most social capital and were the most connected to their gifts and to place.

Keith Basso writes, "Tribes embraced spatial conceptions of history in which places and their names — and all that they symbolize — were accorded central importance. For Indian men and woman, the past lies embedded in features of the earth — the canyons and lakes, mountains and arroyos, rocks and vacant fields — which endow their lands with multiple forms of significance that reach into their lives and the way they think." (Ibid, 1996.)

Early Morning Light:

A Personal Ecoduction

My first memory of the significance of place was the early morning light. The dappled light on the forest floor, the sunlight dancing along the surface of the water, the dust beams caused by light shining through the living room window, the fleeting light at the end of the day, the warmth of the light while sitting with my grandmother on a park bench watching the graceful way the swans looked on water. The light awakened other senses: the intoxicating scent of milkweed, sweetgrass and pine, the wind whispering through the pine boughs, the pebble stones smooth to the touch, the sweet aroma of cherry and peach blossoms, the sound of water washing along the beach, the ominous rumble of thunder just before the first light of dawn.

In my early years, these sense impressions formed a language to explore at the piano. The chipped ivory piano keys were like the smooth curves in the surface of the damp, cool stones I loved to hold as a child. The musty scent of the old upright was reminiscent of the scent of damp leaves on the forest floor. When I feathered the high notes, I became the sunlight dancing on the water's surface.

The piano became the natural extension of my awakening relationship with place. I loved to take a few moments of spontaneous expression and transform it into hours of free play. Music created out of the moment in this way was a precise and organic articulation of what was resonating in the physical and imaginative environment itself. This knowingness of music — sensing this deep current of human feeling — reached into me and expressed a human emotion where words could not go.

Being at the piano, then, particularly in my early years, was an important touchstone for me. It was the place where I could endow my world with significance. I did not relate to the piano as a solo instrument but as an orchestra. Not in a literal sense — I did not consciously think of the upper notes as the flute or the midrange as the cello — but as a full range of tonalities and sonorities that were orchestral in their possibilities. I wanted to release the instrument from its hammers and its percussive tendencies in order to explore its harp-like qualities. I accomplished this by carefully listening to the range of sounds that were possible through the slight adjustment of the weight I placed on the keys and the shape and angle of my hands. In this way, I was a musical painter creating soundscapes, playing all 88 notes as I rendered the images in my imagination into musical adventures on the keyboard.

Because I related to the keyboard as an orchestra, I was inspired and curious about what lay in the spaces between the keys. I loved the experience of my arms and hands outstretched, reaching for the outer extremities of high and low notes of the keyboard like a conductor holding the musicians, the audience and the full surround in the palms of his or her hands. There was no other place in my world where I could so freely take a few moments of spontaneous expression and transform them into hours of delight and free play.

In these moments, it felt as if the full powers of the instrument were alive to my touch and that there was a knowingness that flowed through my arms and shoulders and out through my hands. I was also fortunate to be invited to be the assistant organist at the local church. Here I enjoyed drawing on the choice of orchestral tones with the stops and drawbars to create sacred moods through the extended liturgy of chants and hymns.

I did not know it at the time but, many years later, I would bring these formative experiences at the keyboard into leadership workshops, seminars and large conference environments in the secular world. I would seek to transform these four walls into sacred places by introducing a 'collaborative liturgy' in which people could share a common fellowship through talking, listening and learning together.

The bridge between my private and public life at the piano was also enriched as I created musical soundtracks. When I was young and my friends came to play, they would tell stories or create war games on the living-room rug with beautiful replicas of toy soldiers. I would create soundtracks to the stories and dramas we imagined together.

Sometimes I was so inspired and full of the occasion that I had the sense I was not only playing the piano — I was *being played*. In that moment, the piano was itself a place, and my intention became to create a space of openness and receptivity — a home within myself where it would be possible for this experience of being played to occur again.

I found that same experience of being played at the piano in the beauty of nature. In the presence of beauty, I forgot myself just as I had at the piano, and I had glimpses of something larger, something beyond reach, which gave these experiences a greater sense of power and possibility.

At times, I found this disquieting. There was nothing else in my life experience that supported what I was experiencing in nature and at the piano. In the classroom, our world was composed of discreet, distinct and tangible objects and forms, and we dissected beauty under the microscope.

The enchantment of my world at the piano was quickly reduced to a world of things that cast a shadow on my emerging world of connection and relationships.

Following What is Natural:

The Inner Landscape of Place

What cast this shadow aside was the music of Frederick Chopin. Through Chopin I realized we coexist in both an inner and outer landscape. By nurturing our inner landscapes of place, the contours of our outer world of place also take on a particular shape, rhythm and tone.

I was first introduced to Chopin around the age of 12 when I saw a movie titled *The Eddie Duchin Story.* Eddie Duchin was a widely respected society pianist who opened and closed his engagements with Chopin's "Nocturne in E-Flat Minor." When I heard it performed during the opening scenes, I was completely entranced. I had never heard a piano sound this way before. When I listened to it performed again with two pianos and four hands during the closing scenes, I was overcome with feeling — my eyes filled up with tears. As I left the theatre, I could remember the magnificence of the sonority of the music and the resonance of each musical note.

Chopin was a student of place. His preference for conveying the natural flow and organic form of music revealed how in touch he was with his environment. This intimacy with the natural world meant the refined articulation of the shapes and surfaces of his world were fully embodied in his inner musical articulations. He lived in an empathic resonance with his surroundings.

Not only was he a profound composer, he was also a daring innovator and designer, one whose prophetic harmonies drew succeeding generations of composers and pianists under his spell. In this context Chopin may have been one of our first "ecologists" — a composer and inventor so deeply attuned to his inner and outer environment that his music's deep sensibility served as a touchstone that could detect the most subtle variances in sound, rhythm and pitch.

While my piano lessons had involved precisely following the notes and chords recorded on the page and learning how to interpret the mood and tempo prescribed by the composer, I discovered that, with Chopin, so much more is left for the performer to interpret regarding the structure of sound and space. His interest was always to encourage the student to be guided by his or her own innate sensibility about how the music should flow.

While Chopin's contemporaries were offering virtuosic displays of prodigious speed and technique, Chopin's concept of technique was based on sonority. The mastery of the piano's tonal resources was for him the necessary precursor of virtuosity. To perform Chopin's compositions, therefore, involved exploring all the many ways a note might sound so that you became fully literate in all the tonal possibilities at your fingertips.

For all that Chopin was revered and admired in the world, his music is as much a gift to the performer as to the audience. It is always a deeply personal musical adventure, the articulation a personal touchstone to which everything else can be measured and understood. The seeing, touching and hearing of the music opens an inner landscape in which new qualities of musicality can be felt.

"EASILY EASILY... PLAYING ACCORDING TO YOUR OWN NEED"

Mastering Chopin's language of touch involved less focus on performing from the wrists and the forearms in favour of allowing the sound to begin in the centre of the back. To accomplish this, I needed to be attuned to what felt most natural, including keeping the upper arms and shoulders loose so the elbows could always float free. By shifting my orientation so the whole body was engaged, including my hands, back, shoulders and lungs, I developed a physical and embodied relationship with the instrument.

This enabled me to bring more colour, contour and freedom to my playing so that the upper melodic notes could sing. To find this singing line involved an inner and outer connection. This connection allowed me to develop a suppleness — or *souplesse avant tout!*, as Chopin would say. "Suppleness before everything" was his pianistic motto, and was to be found in the wrist action that gave my hands the flexibility to shape and bend the notes rather than to strike, force or, in Chopin's language, bash them. To Chopin, this was the worst of all offences.

This shift in orientation from playing from the wrists to playing from the whole body was not just a piano technique but a way of living. It was an orientation to the piano that allowed me to more naturally move with the full weight of fingers along the keys, creating both a depth of expression and a lightness of touch. Chopin wanted each finger to find its distinctive character so that the player could expand the full range of their palette. This could not be accomplished if the player yielded to the equalization of the fingers — a common technique at the time. For Chopin, the richness was found in the diversity of the finger weight, rhythm and tone. (2)

Chopin recognized that cultivating these differences through the movement of weight could not be achieved without ease. Ease was at the core of his philosophy of piano technique. This was his trademark prescription — *facilement!* He would say *"easily…easily."* With ease, a pianist could convey the impression of playing with four hands, not just two. Furthermore, when the sound originated from this sense of relaxation and ease, it could unfold freshly and naturally. The piano could speak through the player, and each could play according to their own need.

CHOPIN AND THE ART OF TOUCH

The result of this shift in orientation is that, with Chopin, you don't strike the note. Rather, you develop your own relationship, almost a dance, with the instrument so that you can sink the full weight of your arms and shoulders into how you shape the sound and create a warm singing tone. Chopin looked more for poise and grace in his students' playing than for force or effort. Throughout his teaching, it was the delicacy of the notes that took precedence over technical virtuosity. What he wanted most was for his students to be apprentices to the "art of touch."

"Caress the keys; never force them," he would say repeatedly. And he always encouraged his students to mould each note with a velvet hand rather than striking it — it was as if through immersing themselves in the depths of the piano that the instrument itself was transformed into something alive and responsive to the variability of weight and the expressiveness and intelligence of the hand.

Stiffness exasperated him. He wanted the pianist to play expressively and with ease. To help students find this ease, he would say, "Express as you feel…I give you the full authority to do whatever you want; follow freely the ideal you have set for yourself and which you must feel within you." (Eigeldinger, 1987.)

When playing Chopin, the simplicity and suppleness of the hand and body is the hardest thing. For Chopin, they were also the only thing. No matter how complex or challenging the music, he encouraged his students to approach it with grace. The beautiful quality of sound he sought could only be found by being relaxed at the keyboard. This created the poetry in the sound. It was through the discipline of finding just the right word or image — and his music communicated a kaleidoscope of feelings, stories and images — that he tried to develop a language in which the quality of tone and touch took precedence over speed and virtuosity.

Loving Our Own: Finding Poetry
in Wind and Rain

Every pianistic challenge imaginable is found in the complexity and expressiveness of Chopin's music, and yet at no time did he want his students to strain. Instead, his ultimate goal was for them to connect to their inner music as a touchstone — then, and only then, could they express this music as an intimate articulation of their unique inspiration. Foremost in his mind was the concern that his students avoid the "mental numbness" that comes from too many hours of strenuous practice. "Please," he would say, "to ensure that the spirit of naturalness and simplicity is preserved, if you find yourself straining in your practice, leave the piano alone; instead go for long walks, visit museums or read a good book." This avoidance of stiffness and strain goes to heart of Chopin's teaching and composition.

Aldo Leopold writes, "A thing is right when it tends to preserve the integrity, stability and beauty of the biotic community — it is wrong when it tends to do otherwise." (Ibid, 1999.)

Perhaps what is true in nature holds true in all of life. There was a rightness in Chopin's way of being at the piano. When I followed his lead and trusted what felt most natural within myself, I discovered the integrity, stability and beauty in my playing.

Just as my hands were finding their way along the landscapes of sound, we can also imagine our feet finding their own accommodation as they touch the ground. Touch is a gesture of reciprocity, a way of forming an impression upon and receiving an impression from our world.

Fifty years later, I was again a witness to the music of Chopin in a movie theatre. This time, the movie was *Impromptu*, starring Judy Davis and Hugh Grant. It was set as a lovely period piece in the 1830s outside Paris, where Chopin and his companion, George Sand, are spending a warm Sunday afternoon on a country estate. Suddenly, the rain pours down and they quickly retreat to the parlour where Sand immediately lies under the piano (the only place she would listen to Chopin play) and insists he perform music that has the same feeling of the rain and thunder outside.

The movie brought back to me the place where I first encountered the visceral sounds and sensations of rain and wind. It was while attending a summer camp on the northern tip of Beausoleil Island, a windswept rock scape in the wilderness of Central Ontario on the edge of the wild stormy waters of Georgian Bay. These wonderful granite rocks worn smooth by the waves, with jack pines bent to the winds, offered a unique and marvellous interplay of light and shadow, rock and water, and wind and rain. I was totally captivated by and immersed in this elemental world.

That was really where I discovered how to play — not from the idea of rain, but from the *feeling* and embodiment of it, including the sensation of the power of the wind, the softness of the warm breezes blowing through the white pines, and the dramatic interplay of light and shadow reflected on the water's surface. When the distant rumble of thunder signalled an oncoming storm, I could sense the changing light and feel the vibration of sound in the rock underfoot before I could hear it. That was the summons. I'd go down to the camp lodge, open the screen wide, and play. I played with great passion, as if this was what the natural world was calling me to do.

I didn't play from a musical score; I played from the unique soul of *this* place, the elemental impressions embodied in the windswept waters of Georgian Bay. The art of touch became a personal touchstone, one that started with my first hearing of Chopin's music. It was a quiet ember that burned in my heart through the many years of formal schooling and later on became a source of inner authority I could draw from to find ways of recreating the sound of sensation of wind and rain through the piano keys.

Over the past 20 years, hundreds of people have listened to my musical impressions of wind, rain and thunder in concerts, workshops and presentations. They have also closed their eyes and become immersed in sound; many have even lain side by side under the piano, much as George Sand did 150 years before.

LIFE AS A PILGRIMAGE:

THE UNKNOWABLE LANDSCAPE OF PLACE

Life isn't a project to be completed; it is an
unknowable landscape to be explored.

– David Brooks

Writer David Brooks suggests that life is not the amassing of facts and evidence but rather a pilgrimage in which "we wander across an environment of people and possibilities." (Brooks, 2010.) As we wander, we begin to train our imagination to convey the right signals and also be sensitive to their subtle calls.

Thus, from our earliest days, place, as it was for me being at the piano or immersed in the elemental forces of Georgian Bay, becomes the unknowable landscape that educates and inspires us in how to gaze in wonderment upon the beauty of our world.

Place is not a project to complete; it has no beginning and no end. It is that something other than ourselves, something that holds within it the wildness and preservation of the world we long to explore.

This is what I heard in the music of Chopin — the impression that in every performance there is something fresh and new to be heard:

a subtle turn of phrase, a new harmonic in the chord progressions, a nuance in the melodic line. The notes don't change, but the music is never the same.

This same sense of constant enfoldment, of becoming and dissolving into something else, is available to us all who, through the quality of our continuous attention, become students, admirers and witnesses of place.

Recently in a conference for community leaders in Canada's Atlantic provinces, after reflecting to the music about what place meant for them, participants discovered they shared deep ties to land and sea — and to a mist-filled coastline. Both gentle and unyielding, this sense of place evoked an enduring loyalty to their stories and community. The long history of living on a seabound coast gave them the gift of a perspective larger than any one person or any individual's self-interest. When I heard their stories I was reminded of a line from Annie Proulx's book, *The Shipping News*, in which a young woman, speaking of her father, a cod fisher, said, "He could name a hundred miles of coastline... by the taste of the air."

Similarly, when I asked a group of leaders at Quaker Foods about the significance of place, they found sustenance in their company heritage story and were able to draw on the gifts from its past. Their story had its roots in the founding narrative of their first manufacturing plant in Cedar Rapids, Iowa, and the American heartland. The heartland tale carried a powerful image and association with dedicated work, a sense of integrity, cooperation and self-reliance.

This shared sense of place and story helped them understand and appreciate the common bond of a workplace where personal respect underscored every interaction, where conversations about possibilities thrived, and where all employees were encouraged to discover their own qualities of character and life goals in a manner aligned with the business's core purpose. This strong connection to their heritage enabled them to replicate many aspects of their family culture in their daily work, such as a sense of connection, belonging and pride of place. As one of them said, "Our forefathers created something that has endured through the passage of time — how can we continue to learn from these roots?"

Building Strength
for the Journey:

Elders as Memory-keepers of Place

Father and grandfathers are here
grandmothers and mother
farmers and horsebreakers
tangled in my flesh
who built my strength for the journey.

– Al Purdy, *In the Dream of Myself*

Another important touchstone of place for me, similar to Sherry Lawson's in her story of her elders, were my grandparents. We often first learn of the world through our elders; they become the keepers of the deep memories of place. My grandparents played a vital role, as perhaps only elders can, in initiating me into a deeper awareness of place from their own experiences. Ironically, their story of place had to do with how they found their way in the world after they were uprooted from place and separated from home. Their story also started in Cedar Rapids Iowa.

Both my grandparents, Marion Winter and Ira Needles, had been displaced from their homeland. Each responded to this loss of place in different ways. My grandmother's heart was still in Cedar Rapids and the Iowa farm. Even so, she managed to find ways to make a home and find a place for her heart in her new surroundings. When her growing deafness made day-to-day transactions difficult and a working career impossible, she created a warm and welcoming home with a routine and order that would make it possible for my grandfather to pursue his work in the world. "He does the big things, and I do the little things that make the big things possible," she would say.

Our grandparents and elders in our communities are our memory-keepers of place. They understand and teach us how a relationship to place can give us strength for the journey. Both my grandmother and grandfather had a powerful impact on my life — in very different ways. I will share the stories and lessons from my grandmother first and pick up on my grandfather's story later.

In 1916, my grandmother was the first woman to graduate with a degree in music from Coe College in Cedar Rapids. And while the piano was her first love and her goal was to be a music teacher, her growing deafness through her teenage years limited the scope of what she could hope to achieve.

Because of her deafness, there were many silent transactions between us. Her ability to apprehend the spoken word was limited; she could hear music much more easily. So many of our most important connections were those we made through the keyboard.

The instrument she could hear most clearly was the organ, and she owned two of them. In her home was a Hammond electronic organ with pedals and drawbars, and another, a modest pump organ, was in a small rustic cottage along the sand bars and cedar bush on the eastern shore of Lake Huron. I would play each at every opportunity.

The technique for playing the organ is very different from the piano. With the organ, there is no pedal to sustain the sound of the note being played. Instead, you need to keep your hands on the keys and blend the musical notes. Understanding this, she would take me into the kitchen and have me strengthen my fingers by kneading the bread dough.

It was in this small cottage that I was most influenced by her love for the music of the American heartland that she had left 25 years before. She passed along several songbooks to me. While I worked with the notes, she would share stories of her life on the farm in the Midwest that kept her memory of place alive. Our time together was in the evenings with the sun setting on the far horizon, the flickering of the candles on the organ, the hissing of the kerosene lantern hung from the ceiling, and the steady whine of the mosquitoes on the outside screen.

Sitting beside me on the bench, she would leaf through the pages, randomly selecting songs for me to play. Every song had a story, and as I played she would share these stories with me.

Sometimes late on clear nights, we could hear broadcasters' crackling voices on the shortwave radio. For her, they were voices from home drifting eastward from the Michigan Peninsula, Iowa, and the vast fields of corn and barley that lay farther west. They seemed to be drifting across the wide expanse of this inland sea.

It was she who anchored my sense of the world in the context of a mythic life — a life filled with the awareness of the richness of place, discovered through our connections to our heritage and revealed through language, culture, story, landscapes, ancient gifts and wisdom. This was an archetypal and opaque world — a life behind life — one that has dimmed with the rapid rise of an industrial economy shifting our focus to a more pragmatic view of the future and gradually erasing our connections to our past.

For many, the legacy from the industrial age has been a tsunami sweeping away the footings of connection to their deepest wisdom and true nature. Karen Armstrong writes that, in most pre-industrial cultures, "there were two recognized ways of thinking, speaking and acquiring knowledge. The Greeks called them *mythos* and *logos*. Both were essential and neither was considered superior to the other. They were not in conflict but complementary." (Armstrong, 2009.)

Logos was the voice of reason, and timeless *mythos* the language of the imagination and our felt life together.

With the rise of the industrial economy we found ourselves in a world out of balance. Scientific logos quickly rose to dominance and the mythic life fell into disrepute. With the loss of the mythic life, we no longer had access to the grace and constancy of *ekstasis* — stepping out from the norm and allowing life to live through us so we may experience the ecstasy of our intimate connection to a more enchanted and more-than-human world.

The gift of this inner reality of mythos cannot be retrieved when our worldview is legitimized only in the context of a rational, objective and scientific life. In my grandmother's view, this was leading us toward a 'placeless' world that was out of balance with itself.

Her legacy to me was to set fire my desire, through music, to let life live through me by keeping this mythic world pulsing in my hands and in my heart.

REMEMBERED LANDSCAPES:

THE CONSOLATION OF RECOLLECTED PLACES

The shift from objectivity to receptivity lies at the heart of place-making. And it is through the consolation of recollected places that we discover how the places we once inhabited shape the people we are now.

Robert MacFarlane in his book *The Old Ways; A Journey on Foot* suggests that we tend to think of the landscapes that affect us most strongly as those that are within and around us in present time and with which we connect through sight, sound and touch. But there are also landscapes we carry with us *in absentia*. These places live on in memory long after we have moved on — powerful presences that are lifted up and made even more vibrant through the powers of the imagination.

It was this world, long absent, that my grandmother wanted me to know about — to recognize that these intimate landscapes, altered as they may be by time and distance, were also home to my imagination. As long as I had my life at the piano and in art, I would always know where I came from and never get lost. For it is, as MacFarlane writes, "the consolation of these remembered places, preserved across time, that enlarge and deepen the imagined landscapes we wander in." (MacFarlane, 2012.)

For the early cultures that embraced the mythic life, these spaces *were* their world. They were not threatened by what they could not see or understand; they perceived this mythic dimension as a gift that added richness to their world. And because it was a gift, they believed it was important to practise the ritual of saying thank-you as a way of giving back. They coexisted in partnership with one another in a spirit of deep reciprocity — a stance of open, curious, creative and respectful engagement — knowing that, as they were seeing the world, they were also being *seen by* the world. The awareness of this constant presence of place — that they were not alone — caused them to be in a perpetual state of profound equanimity with their environment.

The shift in our worldview to seeing our environment as a resource to be exploited undermined this equanimity and led to the gradual disenchantment of our world and, subsequently, the permission to take without restraint. However innocent gestures such as unrestricted resource extraction, the intrusion of private land into public spaces and the general disregard of the natural environment may have been at the outset, they quickly escalated into an acquisitional attitude that has come with great cost. This cost becomes even more apparent as we discover what we've lost when we learn to see our world through not only an economic but also an ecological lens.

As the transmitter of beauty, place instils a longing that draws us back toward these places of meaning in our life. It was seeing the beauty of place, the long horizon and light-filled wide-open skies through my grandmother's eyes, that inspired my own exploration of an open and spacious style of playing at the keyboard.

With her growing deafness — but deep musical sense — she introduced me to a more sentient way of knowing the world. She shared with me how we come into the awareness of place through its particularities. Too often, the mark of the world of logos is to become an immoveable object; in order to study something, we believe we must maintain our separateness, objectivity and sense of detachment and not be moved by what we see. We attempt to diminish and demystify our subjective experience in order to reduce the full presence of place so it can't influence or touch us in any way.

Finding Faith in Fragments:

Nurturing an Observance of Our World

My grandmother's mythic relationship to the world of place was the opposite. To her, studying the world meant entering into an empathic resonance with place, to connect to its memories, its heritage, its beauty and its craft, in each moment. She believed that the true gift of place is that it helps us see and connect in this larger, deeper way. Instead of seeing only discreet, distinct and tangible forms — a form of observation that reduces and divides our world into separate compartments and objects — she looked at the world as a whole and appreciated the glimmers and possibilities that lay just beyond what could be clearly seen.

Her patterns of observance find their echo in the words of Kim Stafford, whose father, William Stafford, wrote poetry that also found deep resonance in the distant horizons of the American Midwest: "We tend to receive glimmerings, hints, occasional fragments, and quiet insights…this is why we are required to honour small moments of learning, to have faith in fragments and over time to quilt our solitudes into whole structures." (K. Stafford, 2003.)

This way of relating to the world leads us to see deeply into the other. It asks us to look beyond the superficial impressions of light, wind and sky, or the general features of a plant or tree, to see the 'deep inscape,' the rich details, patterns, rhythms and movements of imaginative sight. Those particulars that our senses take in are lifted up and amplified by the imagination, which makes these images even more vivid and whole.

In learning to regard the particularities in the other, we also see the gifts and essence of the other — and they in us. This may help account for place-based communities being also gift-sharing and vocational communities. With imaginative sight, we cannot see a place without also seeing the gift of place. This gift of place invites a sense of mutual evocation so that, when we walk the land and let it speak to us, we feel gratitude for the gifts of insight and peace we have taken from it. It is this shift from objectivity to reciprocity that lies at the heart of placemaking and participating in a place-based world.

E. V. Walter in his book *Placeways* suggests that this reciprocity finds its roots in the Greek word *haptein*. It is a word that has no equivalent in the English language but represents the sense of touch — both of touching and being touched by the world — not only with the hand but also with the whole body and all the senses. It is a perceptual process that includes the whole body-mind experience of pressure, warmth and kinesthesia.

This *haptic* sense enlivens a way of being that finds its roots in our archaic past, when we literally *felt* the world in our bones. It is a way we grasp our reality not only in our seeing and hearing but in ways considered more primitive, such as through our feelings, rhythm, touch, vibration and flow. Through these more elemental senses, we discover what it means and how it feels to dwell in and inhabit a place — perhaps for the first time.

In the years I sat with my grandmother, I was reminded of how much I lived in a two-fold universe. One universe resonated with the mythic life of art, creativity, landscape and the enchantment of place. The other, encompassed by my formal education and my growing interest in leadership, organizations, communities and higher education, was in a world of logos somewhat removed from the more enchanted world she was introducing me to.

If my grandmother's place was in nature and the recollected mythic stories from the past that she carried from the American heartland, my grandfather was a man of science whose place was in the future and the fulfillment of his own vision of transforming higher education in Canada.

As I mentioned earlier, my grandparents left family farms at an early age to attend university. When they graduated from Coe College in Cedar Rapids, Iowa, my grandfather went on to attend Northwestern University in Evanston, Illinois, where he completed a postgraduate fellowship in business administration. He then began working with BF Goodrich in 1916 in Akron, Ohio, and later in New York City.

When they arrived in Kitchener, Ontario, in 1924, my grandfather took a job as assistant sales manager at BF Goodrich Canada. He concealed the fact that he was university educated. The town (which was then called Berlin) was not open to strangers and particularly Americans. At that time, the business world also considered it elitist to have a degree in higher education. Despite these difficulties and perhaps because he still carried the humbleness of his farm background in his heart, he was well liked. He gradually rose within the ranks of the tire giant and by 1951 he was appointed president of BF Goodrich Canada.

By the summer of 1956, my grandfather had established a life in two worlds: industry and academia. These two worlds would finally come together in a radical speech he made to the Rotary Club of Kitchener-Waterloo that year — a speech that would ultimately transform the nature of education in Canada. During his talk, entitled "WANTED: 150,000 Engineers: The Waterloo Plan," my grandfather presented a new vision for education that would involve studies in the classroom as well as training in industry. The goal was to educate skilled engineering graduates to fill a need in the rapidly expanding industrial hub around Kitchener-Waterloo. But for him, it was something larger than that.

He had a dream for the university to be the hub for a new kind of technological ecosystem. He foresaw that the energy for transformational change comes from place, and particularly at the intersection of two or more places. It was his goal to get universities, industry and civil society working together to fill this growing need. And in 1957, with the encouragement and help of a close BF Goodrich colleague, Gerald Hagey, he founded the University of Waterloo (UW).

His thoughts on cooperative education, while controversial at the time, eventually helped place the University of Waterloo among the top-tier global universities and set the standard for cooperative education in North America. This would have been hard to imagine the day he sunk a spade into the ground of an open cornfield north of Kitchener. Yet his pragmatic approach to education would counter the historic reality of universities being restricted to the privileged classes. In its place he envisioned a community-based university that could also serve the global community as a hub — an incubator and accelerator — for large-scale innovation and change. In so doing he was also imagining and crafting a future that would not be realized within his own lifetime.

One of the products of his vision, although he could not see it in detail at the time, was RIM and BlackBerry. Not only was RIM a Waterloo-based global leader in cell phone technology for over a decade, it also contributed to creating 1,000 other technology start-ups in the region that employ tens of thousands of innovators, inventors and technologists.

"As the Needles name suggests, he had a way of getting people moving," one official said of my grandfather. "And the reason is simple: he didn't care very much who got the credit for it."

He was influenced, as he said to me, by his early years on the family farm immersed in the annual cycles of germination, growth, decay and new birth. This experience instilled a sense of patience and humility in the face of changes on a large scale so that, as in nature, no one person could take full credit for everything that unfolded.

As former UW president Bert Matthews said, "He was not only a member of that small group of men who met... to consider the possibility of establishing a university here; he was also the guiding light, the spark plug if you like, that ignited the enthusiasm of the whole group." After helping to found the university, he went on to serve as chairman of its board of governors between 1956 and 1966 before being appointed Chancellor — a position he served until his late 80s.

My grandfather was a man of logos, full of ideas, possessing a keen intellect and a deep grounding in academics and business, and a thoughtful and visionary leader with a clear sense of strategy and a prophetic vision. Yet it was my grandmother's sense of life's mythic dimension of hearth and home, her empathy, imagination, story-telling and appreciation for poetry, nature, beauty and the aesthetic sense — even her growing deafness — that made the success of my grandfather's logos possible. When I joined them for conversation, I noticed the care with which my grandfather would repeat certain phrases or speak slowly, and a little more loudly, to correct misunderstandings and to be sure she understood and was included in all I had said. I also remember when he would pause and let his attention be drawn to a story or a poem — something that reconnected him to his own sense of home.

This quality of listening and inclusion seemed to underscore his artfulness in bringing different groups together, of building consensus, of resilience and focus, of faith in others, and enrolling them in his vision through his story-telling and empathy. In these ways, he displayed the qualities learned from my grandmother and the generations before them who worked and learned from the earth together.

When I reflect on the sense of place in the context of my grandparents' lives, they appear to have been working with tensions common in balancing two contradictory impulses in relation to place. For my grandfather, the forces at work were about mobility and moving forward. His sense of destiny took flight as he envisioned creating a home for others in the future. For my grandmother, it was about rooting and delving downward. She offered the soil that supported my grandfather's vision to reach toward a larger unknown.

Edward Thomas, himself a poet, journeyer and dedicated student of place, writes that the stability of the forest and the mobility of the path are the two most distinctive features of landscape. The roots that delve down and the step that moves outward serve as two contrasting metaphors for our connection with the world. (MacFarlane, 2012.) These two forces, including the forward movement of logos and the downward rootedness of mythos, together offer the possibility of both prophetic leadership and a balanced life.

A world dominated by logos is a world out of balance. For all that is accomplished, it is a world that may have more builders than nesters, more takers than leavers, and more mobility and displacement than dwelling and belonging.

It is hard to make anything like a truce between these two incompatible desires, Thomas wrote. "The one going on and on over the earth, the other would settle forever in one place…"

But together they offer integration, a blending together of the body, mind and heart that seems essential for creating a place-based life.

Bringing Vision to Flower:

The Generosity of a Place-based Life

"Nobody sees a flower really; it is so small. We haven't time,
and to see takes time – like to have a friend takes time."

– Georgia O'Keefe

As I listened to my grandfather during those formative years and observed him tracing the unknowable landscape from industrialist/manager to businessman/leader to steward/visionary and builder, it was clear that it was not finance and economics that fired his imagination. He was an example of a new kind of leader, one who thinks beyond the numbers and the short term to envision and create a place for future generations ahead. He knew that his vision could not be fulfilled within his own lifetime — a perspective somewhat uncommon for the more typical business leaders who focused primarily on skills, tools and outcomes in the short term.

True to his agrarian past and my grandmother's focus on creating a place of dwelling, he could see the flower, no matter how small, where others could see only dust and dirt. He could see the possibilities, unharvested and untended — fertile soil others may not have taken the time to look for.

His grounding in place and placemaking guided him in not only thinking about bricks and mortar but also looking deeper to craft incubators, networks and relationships across sectors and imagining them coming into full flower. His foresight in acquiring vast acreages of land — land that even now is not in full use — reflected the breadth of his vision: one building evolving into a large, complex living system that could accommodate the full scope of the dreams he and others held for it through the fullness of time.

To the extent we carry our place inside us and recreate it wherever we go, it is possible my grandfather created a little of Iowa in the Waterloo region as well. As one co-op graduate said to me, "The co-op program and the university are like a farm. We come here to grow and incubate ideas for eight months, and then we go out into the world for four months and plant our seeds, and then we come back and incubate some more." (4)

And this is the generosity of a place-based life.

My grandfather could not return to the Iowa farm. But he could translate those early experiences of place into an aspiration to recreate that same complex ecosystem in another time and another place. He did not necessarily see the University of Waterloo based on grades and curriculum; instead, he envisioned it in ways that were consistent with how nature thinks — as an environment made fertile by nurturing a network of relationships and connectivity, complex and interconnected root systems capable of incubating craft-based innovative technologies and growing engineering talent that could collaborate and learn alongside the best in the world.

When I think about place in the context of my grandparents, several aspects become clear.

Place is Living Generously

Our relationship to place evokes a particular kind of wisdom about living generously and living well. Place teaches us about empathy and perceiving deeply, processes that are inherently slow. Place is a remedy to the stress of having to cope in a fast-paced world.

Place is a Sanctuary

Place satisfies a human hunger rarely met in our modern age. Many people, even those who seem settled and deeply rooted in a place, have a sense of being lost or orphaned in a placeless world. This longing reminds us how place offers solace as a sanctuary for stories and a source of inspiration, of hospitality and belonging in uncertain times.

Place is a Conversation

For a place to be a place we need to be in relationship with it — a place is not an object or thing but a conversation. Words spoken out of a sense of place are prophetic in that they express a vision and a story that is different from the utilitarian language of quotas and rules. In a place-based world, leaders and consultants become poets and sages, and language becomes less a tool to inform and more a force of transformation.

Place is a Pilgrimage

While space represents a form of escape like a weekend holiday or retreat — a neutral space — place holds historical roots and associations; places tell stories of beginnings and a pilgrimage into an unknown future as we search for home and where we most belong. The significance of these stories is that tracing our own path to finding our place matters — it is where our own sense of destiny may be found.

Place is Something to Grow out From

Place is not only something to return to but something to grow out from. Place teaches us about love and particularly about how to love not only one place but many places. When we love one place deeply, it is never forgotten. It becomes a force of nature that strengthens our ability to discover how to love other places later on.

Place Keeps Possibility Alive

The mystery of what makes a place a place evokes an appreciation of beauty, which keeps hope and possibility alive. Through place, we learn to make a home for ourselves in the world. Place is a gift, and as a gift it reflects back to us the beauty within ourselves and in our own life and work.

LEADERSHIP AS CRAFT:

FILLING SPACE IN A BEAUTIFUL WAY

We have lost the art of making things and filling space in a beautiful way.

In a world in which many feel out of place, we need to look to leaders who see their leadership practice in the context of place and placemaking. We need to understand more about their unique contributions to leadership practice and how we might emulate them. We might ask these questions:

- What are the heartfelt aspirations and sense of destiny that differentiate these transformative leaders from others?

- How does the sense of being uprooted and the longing for home inspire them? How does place inspire those who have not experienced this sense of uprootedness and separation?

- How does a sense of craft and filling spaces in a beautiful way serve as one of the principles that inform their vision and lead them to being place-based leaders?

- How does their own story of place become something to grow out from so they may learn to see the gifts and deep potential in others?

- How has their love of place inspired them to nourish a culture of neighbourhoods in the workplace, including a sense of belonging and care?

- And how does a sense of place teach leaders about balancing the energies of mythos and logos in their own life and work? That includes slowing down to see the flower and — through the power of this image — imagine what it is they most wish to bring to full flower in their life and in their work.

It is through the exploration of these questions that we may bring about a renaissance in leadership practice.

PART THREE

READING THE FIELD:

The Artful Landscapes of Place

We stand at the threshold of a future we can neither predict nor control. In the presence of such uncertainties the leader's role shifts from managing discrete parts to reading the field and the emerging patterns of the whole. It is a time when leaders will see their work as craft and their world as a dynamic field of energy characterized by constantly evolving patterns of relationship and flow. With this resurgence of craft, leaders will have opportunities to design and shape their future not only with their minds but with their hands and with their hearts.

ROOTS OF ALIVENESS:

THE ART OF REGENERATIVE LEADERSHIP

*Even tomato plants and the tallest trees send down roots
as they rise towards the light. Yet the metaphors for our
lives see mainly the upward part of organic motion.*

– James Hillman

We cannot manage or plan our way into an unknown future, but we can be led. We can apprentice ourselves to a master craftsman who can fire our imagination with an inner knowing that cannot be formally taught but only acquired through imitation and experience. And with this same imagination we can also master the ability to focus on the far horizon while holding to the ground we are standing on at the same time.

It has been said that the span of our awareness is a mile wide and an inch deep. The quality of our deep life is frequently overlooked in our efforts to cope with the surface demands and expectations of our outer life.

To understand what differentiates leaders who nurture their inner life, we might take as our point of reference the image of an oak tree. Trees have always served as wisdom teachers — reminders that the upward push of a career needs to be balanced with planting our feet firmly in the ground of the places we live and come from. As George Bernard Shaw once said, "no one manages their affairs as well as a tree does."

Leaves and branches symbolize the first level of learning and change. These represent the busyness of the day-to-day with the focus on tactics, action plans, performance goals, desired outcomes and results. If we direct our attention down a little, to the trunk and lower limbs, we begin to look at structures, strategies and processes.

Soil and the root systems are at the third level. The regenerative nature of roots and soil give the tree the resilience and strength to grow. The fertility of the soil is critical in enabling the acorn to realize its destiny as a sturdy oak, able to weather sudden changes year after year. Yet we spend the least amount of our time focused on the ground underneath the tree.

This brief overview offers a framework for making distinctions between these three levels of leadership and learning in organizations and communities.

LEVEL 1:

TECHNICAL/TACTICAL

At this first level, the focus is on utility, events and *action*. The primary question is, "How do we *do* things differently?"

In the tree metaphor, Level 1 learning takes into account the flowering and foliage of the branches and the leaves and how the energy of the sun contributes to the harvesting of events, action and results. It frames the organization as a mechanical system for which all problems have a corresponding technical, expert-driven response. If this level prevails in an organization, everything is consumed; nothing is conserved for the future. As such, Level 1 learning is reactive to the short-term environment and vulnerable to changing circumstances. Because this level is focused on the performance of the parts rather than the system as a whole, it emphasizes what is most immediate and visible, which contributes to efficiency-based thinking, quantitatively driven results and mechanistic expert-driven solutions.

Very often this level of leadership is like managing in a bubble. A course of action is chosen in reaction to external circumstances rather than with a proactive vision from within of what we want to create.

While it is important to acknowledge that the leaves take in energy from the sun and transfer this to the tree, forms of energy transfer that come from other sources underground are often overlooked.

LEVEL 2:

STRATEGIC/TRANSACTIONAL

Here, the primary focus is on strategy, process and *meaning*. The question is, "How do we do *different* things?"

This second level of learning involves seeing not only the leaves and branches but how their support is dependent upon the resilience, structural integrity and strength of the trunk. Although Level 2 learning shifts the emphasis from efficiency to effectiveness, it doesn't necessarily ask the larger, higher-order questions such as effectiveness to what end? The focus in Level 2 learning is on interpersonal or transactional strategic-based learning. The predominant language is meaning, planning, concepts and control. The focus is on process, structure and effectiveness. Measurement is qualitative, and there is a greater reliance on emotional intelligence and teamwork.

But the focus is still on preservation rather than generation and focusing on the parts rather than building networks of relationships with the whole. For this, we need to look to another level of learning that is associated more with a perceptual shift and with deeper levels of engagement.

LEVEL 3:

REGENERATIVE/TRANSFORMATIONAL

With regenerative Level 3 learning, the primary focus is *feeling*, tone, beauty and adaptivity. The primary question is, "How do we *see* differently?"

The focus at Level 3 is on the shift from mechanistic, parts-based thinking to place-based thinking that engages the ecology of the whole organization as a living system where complex questions of beauty, meaning and purpose can be explored and acted upon. If the other levels focus on meaning and action, Level 3 learning examines beauty. This is because beauty lies at the root of things. Like the roots of the tree, beauty nourishes everything else.

To be regenerative means to be participative, reciprocal and imaginative. It involves focusing on the tonal qualities, the atmosphere, the energy dynamics and flow of the system. This includes doing things that move beyond the status quo of preserving the life of the tree to fulfilling as well as ensuring the health of the forest as a whole.

Root systems as antennae and receptors are infinitely alive — inquiring, sensing, absorbing, inventing and changing course in the moment — as they feel their way. In their search for connectivity and fertile ground, roots are also infinitely adaptive and improvisational, seeking new possibilities for the tree to transform nourishment into new growth.

The focus of leadership shifts from exploiting nature as an object or resource separate from us to seeing nature as a powerful repository of memories, dreams and associations with which we can bring our own sense of destiny alive.

Place and placemaking serve as the ground for our vision of possibility taking root and growing. Place also teaches us about beauty and how beauty keeps our sense of hope and possibility alive. And beauty teaches us how to create safe environments — or sanctuaries — for identifying and nurturing the important work that needs to be done in the world.

When we look at these three levels, they represent distinctions in how we lead and communicate as well as how we learn. They also reflect three distinct worldviews. In a few short decades, we have begun to see our worldview shift: Level 1, representing an industrial mindset in which the natural world is an unlimited and exploitable resource for us to consume; to Level 2, a sustainability mindset in which the natural world is finite requiring preservation if we are to survive and thrive; to Level 3, an emerging worldview in which the natural world is an intelligent and life-generating force key to our future. To come into an alignment with this force will involve the fundamental shift from thinking as machines think to thinking as technology thinks to thinking as nature thinks.

Shifting our focus to Level 3 — thinking as nature thinks — helps us change our perspective. With Level 1 and Level 2 learning, the emphasis is on the self-referential "I." As a consequence, we often are conditioned to patterns of thought that cause us to repeat what worked in the past. As ecologist David Orr writes, "Many of our current problems stem from past success carried to an extreme." (Orr, 2002.)

With regenerative Level 3 learning, we develop a new kind of reflective sight — an insight with the self-aware eye. As I will explore in the next section, the self-aware eye is similar to the eye of the artist whose attention to craft shifts their focus from themselves and their immediate or past circumstances to the present moment and materials at hand.

With this mindset, instead of asking "What should I do?" we ask, "What is the work *asking* me to do?" When we engage with the first question, we find we are focused on the doing, including our expectations regarding what should happen. This may be out of step with what is already in process and wants to happen naturally. To re-engage, we need to see ourselves not as observers but as collaborative partners, aligned in the co-creation of outcomes emerging in the moment and seeking to create and sustain life.

In this context, we need to explore a new framework that is not only life-consuming or life-preserving but *life-generating*. This approach asks not only how we do the best we can with what we have left, but how to fill a space with something that did not exist even a moment before.

This approach to leadership focuses not only on preservation, based on what we accrued in the past, but co-generation as pioneers, engaging the imagination and creating out of the moment so we can make our world anew.

An Ever-Breaking Newness:

The Underpinnings of
Place-based Learning and Change

Our ideas are like seeds. To flourish, when we harvest, we must not consume them all but turn some back to the earth to be transformed to compost in order to further enrich the soil. Out of one idea grows another . . . and that also is turned under. The seeds that are finally offered are the result of a patient waiting upon the gift – and it grows in response to the months of patient turning and building of the soil.

– Robert Frost in Jay Parini's *Robert Frost – A Life*, 1999

This source of new life is in the roots and soil. Eighty percent of what determines the health of a tree is the condition of the black magic beneath the surface. In the context of an organization, this black magic is found in our art, our gifts, our sense of ownership, collaboration and empowerment and our unexplored possibilities. Together these are the growing places where the seeds of our future are silently building strength for what Robert Frost called our "ever breaking newness." A newness that may be heard in the conversations we have not yet had.

We tap into this black magic when we engage in conversations and stories that get at the root of things. When we shift from passive questions that require yes or no responses to reflective questions that truly and authentically engage the other, we awaken the self-aware eye and, with this, a new way of seeing. To tap into these root conversations, we may ask each other

- What do you most deeply aspire to create?

- When do you feel most vital, alive and rejuvenated as a leader?

- How do you cope with your own vulnerability and uncertainty?

- How have you found the inner courage to overcome a perceived obstacle?

- Can you think of a story of a place that inspired you and your leadership?

These deeper tonal questions brush aside the surface cover in order to get at stories and images in the undergrowth that is at the root of what it means to be truly alive. They tap into the generative power of a metaphorical or symbolic language rooted in an ancient perception, based on our felt experience and not only on analysis and abstract thought.

Aldo Leopold writes, "Land is not merely soil; it is an energy circuit that native plants and animals keep open while others may or may not." (Leopold, 1999.)

In a similar vein, root questions tap into this native energy circuit of place that helps to keep open our appreciation of what leadership is for. Root questions offer up a language of buried meanings and feelings that, when explored and more deeply felt, help us build deep connections at a more visceral level.

To make these connections, we need to shift our speaking from reporting what is already formed to digging deep for words that carry the intuitive truths — to discover a language that is not absolute but generative, words that are not decreed but form on the tongue as we speak.

American author Willa Cather, like Aldo Leopold, acquaints us with this sense of the underlying current of energy infusing a living and sentient landscape when she writes how a man could grow young in the presence of a wind rich with the fragrance of "hot sun, sagebrush and sweet clover; a wind that made one's body feel light and one's heart cry 'To-day, to-day,' like a child's." (Cather, 1927.)

She noticed how this particular quality vanished after the land "was tamed by man and made to bear harvests." Somehow, this heaviness of labour, growth and grain-bearing burdened the soil. "...one could breathe that only on the bright edges of the world," on the perpetual flowering of "the great grass plains and the sage-brush desert." (Ibid, 1927.)

This notion of the landscape being a current of energy is also vividly portrayed by traveller Nan Shepherd when she writes, "As I watch [the world] it arches its back, and each layer of landscape bristles." (*The Living Mountain*, Nan Shepherd, 2011.)

The words of Leopold, Cather and Shepherd, each in their own way, relay close observations of the underpinnings of place and its effect on us. They offer reminders that place is not a noun but a verb. As such, it cannot be fully appreciated from a distance. Place itself is alive — an active, vibrant participant that bristles in our presence.

When we share questions and stories that get at the roots of things, the room itself bristles. Root systems act out of a similar alchemy — a force of attraction — that leads them to commingle, creating complex latticework beneath the soil. Root systems know that the nutrients they seek — like the creative streams of curiosity and attraction themselves — are not evenly distributed but concentrate in particular places. So roots seek those locations where soil conditions are most alive. Root systems have the uncanny ability to transfer nutrients in the form of moisture to support the health of the whole without diminishing their own health and well-being.

When we attempt to tame our world, we may inadvertently diminish the life force that created it. This reality is vividly portrayed in *New York Times* columnist Timothy Egan's 2006 book, *The Worst Hard Time*. His story brings home the fragility of our existence: despite our many accomplishments, we are nature. As nature, we owe our existence to the six-inch layer of topsoil beneath our feet.

In a world where we have assumed that the much-needed rains are a constant, Egan writes about what happens when it doesn't rain:

> The Dust Bowl is literally a story about roots — a century ago, large sections of the American plains were plowed up, ostensibly to make them more fertile and productive. Tragically, this was done without consideration of the value of the delicate fabric of groundcover — literally, an organic carpet of interlocking prairie grasses — which had evolved over long periods of time to become the foundation for all life on the plains... in the spring, this carpet of grass flowered amid the green, and as the wind blew, it looked like music on the ground.
>
> ...Aside from its obvious role as habitat and primary food source, the latticework of a variety of different grasses was the anchor of life against the constant wind. It held the soil in place, allowing life to have a foothold in an otherwise hostile environment. The interstitching of modest life forms made everything else possible. When they were gone, there was nothing to stop the

wind, and it took everything in its path: crops, people, houses, towns, and the civilization they represent.

Egan, like Robert Frost before him, foresaw the same "dark dust cloud" on the horizon: when the roots of place are ploughed under by competing economic and market interests, there is also a loss of the creative vitality for building a sustainable future.

Creative communities are also composed of a delicate and interconnected latticework of root structures: neighbourhoods, associations, networks and relationships. Too often we believe that these time-honoured relationships are inexhaustible, just as the farmers on the plains believed the soil was indestructible. As long as the weave of grass is stitched to the land and the roots remain moist and alive while dormant during the driest years, the land can — and did — flourish for thousands of years. But when the sod was turned, the roots were upended and exposed to the dry air and hot sun, and in less than one generation, the land had died at the hands of those who'd hoped to prosper on it.

We participate in moistening the roots and building soil every time we bring our gifts to the work of community. Just as the attraction of seeds to soil brings the land alive, our gifts bring places and communities alive. Each is a powerful attractor for the other. Digging for words connects us to the roots of our own vitality. It forms the latticework and root structure of human community. We don't just talk; we are brought to speech. Together, these root conversations tap into the inherent wealth that is present when we consciously build and deepen our relationships with one another. They create the fertile ground — ground frequently passed over in our fast-paced lives — where the seeds of our future can take root and grow.

Level 3 regenerative leadership and learning relies on this inner felt sense that accesses the invisible root structures for whole mind and holistic learning. Our focus shifts from technical and transactional matters to complex transformative learning. Our practice field shifts from management and leadership to stewardship — being gardeners tending to the well-being of the dynamics of the whole. We also extend our imagination across boundaries to other systems in order to see the larger unfolding patterns that connect our communities to a systemic sensing of the whole of life.

Most importantly, our internal rhythm shifts from clock time to organic time. From the beginning, our universe has been expanding at just the right rate necessary for life to emerge. As such, we live in a life-generating universe. It represents a complex interplay of forces of expansion and contraction that are elegantly designed to support life.

The shift from Level 1 and Level 2 to Level 3 learning reflects a similar shift in our relationship to time. In the first two levels, we live by mechanical or clock time. In this brightly illuminated world, time is our adversary; we feel we rarely have enough time to achieve our ends. By watching the clock, our surroundings fade from view; we don't have the time to be conscious of the places we are in.

In Level 3 learning, our relationship to time slows down. We cross a threshold into timeless time, where we become absorbed in our world in ways that make time stand still. In this moment, we have entered regenerative, or craft, time — an experience of time out of time where our sense of place is heightened and our world itself may be transformed.

GROWING WHILE LOOKING:

LEARNING TO SEE OUR WORLD ANEW

Observe, observe this river of life flowing through your
existence – if you fail to grasp it, it will elude you.

– Michel de Montaigne

It is commonly believed that the fastest way to change a system is with Level 1 (Technical/Tactical) and Level 2 (Strategic/ Transactional) actions. The majority of an organization's attention is usually focused on these two areas. Yet from what we are learning in our exploration of time, the typical goal-setting processes that emphasize specific, measurable, achievable, realistic and time-bound results rarely correlate with either work satisfaction, efficiency or success.

While they are highly charged, time-driven and activity-based, Level 1 and Level 2 learning rarely produce long-term, sustainable change on their own. Both technical and strategic thinking tend to get wrapped up in the details. They fixate on objects, fixed categories and data-driven ways of thinking that divert our attention from the more powerful patterns of unfolding meaning and imaginative insight that shapes the complex root systems of our organizations and communities.

Donella Meadows, in her article "Places to Intervene in a System," states that the slowest way to change a system is with numbers. "Diddling with the details is like re-arranging the deck chairs on the Titanic," she says. So much of our attention goes to numbers, but there's not a lot of power in them. Too often the discussion is simply about addressing the status quo in a more efficient or effective manner. (Meadows, 1997.)

While it may be counterintuitive, the fastest way to change a system is by changing the mental model or worldview out of which the system arises. "You could say paradigms are harder to change than anything else about a system, and therefore, this item should be lowest on the list, not the highest," Meadows writes. "But for a single individual, it can happen in a millisecond. All it takes is a click in the mind, a new way of seeing. Of course, individuals and societies do resist challenges to their paradigm harder than they resist any other kind of change." (Ibid,1997)

While we need to be highly literate with Level 1 and Level 2 learning, we also must be aware of their limitations. They concentrate our attention on the most obvious and visible issues. They promote an expert-driven "outside in" response that rarely evokes a fundamental shift of mind when practiced without the broader and sometimes counterintuitive insights that come from Level 3 learning.

Very often, Level 1 and Level 2 learning involves grasping at simple actionable solutions to complex issues. They also tend to be overly reliant on external indicators such as cost reductions, quarterly profits, competitor benchmarking and customer research. Too often, these "objective" indicators contribute to maintaining the status quo and distract or override what leaders intuitively know to be true.

When we focus on these external indicators, we may actually impede the growth of the system as a whole.

To come to a greater awareness of what is needed, we cannot rely solely on solutions from the outside. Leaders also need to trust their own intuition, felt sense, and the local wisdom of the community and the place they serve. While all levels of learning are necessary, only Level 3 learning and regenerative leadership invite us into an artful and imaginative conversation with the future. It takes technical and strategic learning in new directions that could not have been foreseen in advance.

By thinking locally and globally at the same time, Level 3 leaders are able to meet challenges and opportunities that are generally impossible for any individual to handle on their own. Rosabeth Moss Kanter, a widely recognized opinion-shaper in the areas of strategy, innovation and leadership, suggests that the pursuit of innovation usually involves studying the great leaders who think outside the box. But the leaders we need to be studying, she suggests, are those advanced leaders who go even further and think *outside the building*.

LEADERS AS BOUNDARY-CROSSERS:

CREATING SOCIAL FIELDS FOR LEARNING

I am not a businessman; I am an artist.

– Warren Buffet

These advanced — or what I have been referring to as *regenerative* — leaders are boundary-crossers. As Warren Buffet suggests, they are artists who understand how to lead along the ecotones — or narrow pathways — where ecologies are held in a creative tension.

They understand intuitively that these points of intersection, or boundary crossings, represent places that vibrate at a higher intensity. Being grounded in a sense of place helps define who they are, where they come from and what makes them unique. This gives them the acumen to attend to the details of business and also see the world as craftspeople, designers and artists. Their grounding in place enables them to think beyond the defined mandates, goals and actions of their organization or community to reach out and build regional and global coalitions and communities.

What distinguishes these boundary-crossers is that they are able to, in the words of former United Nations Secretary Kofi Annan, jump levels. That is, they are able to focus on a micro level and balance the practicalities of an economic worldview and also jump to a macro level, where they have an ecological whole-system perspective. They understand how to position their organizations not only in the marketplace but also at the social nexus in which sectors overlap and societal problems and solutions become a part of the commons and so belong to everyone. Like performing in an improvisational ensemble, they are adept at listening for the unfolding of the whole while at the same time attending to their part as it emerges.

Like my grandfather, who jumped levels as he shifted from being a manager and industrialist to realizing a destiny that would bring academia, civil society and industry together, regenerative leaders are artists and mythmakers in that they see their world with fresh eyes each and every day. They understand the broader context in which they operate and have the vision to change it. By adding societal and educational values to financial outcomes, these leaders can create long-term, meaningful human institutions out of what Kanter describes as a bundle of "impersonal assets." They transform these impersonal assets into social capital, using them to fulfill the needs of the disadvantaged and future generations.

Perhaps because he came from outside the community, my grandfather sensed the potential in the social field through its deep skill base and potential as well as the entrepreneurial spirit that had been a part of its identity and heritage since the city was founded in 1816. He tapped into this to articulate the Waterloo Plan, which over time would evolve into the Waterloo Way.

He tapped into these core strengths through building first upon the community's deep mythic roots and civic pride that had been an integral part of its founding Mennonite, Germanic and British cultural traditions. In this way, he accessed the community's deeply rooted, craft-based manufacturing heritage that could — and often did — reinvent itself. (Seagrams, for example, founded in 1857, was for a time the largest distillery in the world. Later came Electrohome, a multinational maker of home stereos, and later still came RIM, the maker of the BlackBerry.)

He accessed the community's freewheeling entrepreneurship in order to create fertile ground for its cooperative educational programs and high-tech start-up industries. In other words, he articulated a vision aligned with the community's unique story of place and its local traditions rooted in a dedicated craft-based culture. He built upon that to form an even greater sense of its identity. Together, these start-up enterprises, like bright, rich, green shoots of plants, created a place that, as one co-op graduate said, "was uniquely capable of supporting its citizens through strong connections and a maverick spirit, entrepreneurship and self-reliance." (5)

Through the strength of their vision, regenerative leaders draw from the local wisdom, collective intelligence and uniqueness of the places they find themselves. In turn, they create environments that are expressions of the community's aspirations and greater destiny.

Leadership that is ecologically minded and place-based is the new story of the future.

This perspective gives leaders the tools to engage in a larger unknown and speak about what is often difficult to express. It helps them appreciate that to lead outside the building is to lead without a script. It requires a generative conversation around those questions that tap into the vitality and aliveness of the root system of the organization or community and build a storyline sufficiently bold for others to want to belong to it. It invites leaders to speak authentically about experiences that can be contained not in a linear flashlight world of spreadsheets and strategic plans but in the candlelight world of mystery, paradox, complexity and surprise.

The concept of flashlight and candlelight is relevant in understanding our relationship to place. While we most often rely on the flashlight to illuminate, its blinding light frequently impairs our ability to see. While it may appear counterintuitive, to see our world clearly we need all our senses to be alert to the opaqueness of our surroundings — a way of seeing that clarifies our vision even more when shrouded in the flickering of candlelight.

In this context my grandfather learned something about place and leading generatively from my grandmother. Her hearing impairment meant she had to live in a candlelight world — one in which her limitations in one area required her to compensate by living at the periphery of the day-to-day world. I believe she helped him understand that he belonged not only to a profession and a career but also to a story and a place.

She contributed to his understanding that it was his calling to create a sense of destiny not only for himself but for the larger community. She knew that, in order to act wisely in a turbulent world where there are no fixed rules, no broad consensus and no clear way forward and where signals could be both confused and conflicting, he would need to know his story of place. This would help him stay grounded and focused on where he wanted to influence and inspire others.

This grounding is particularly necessary for leaders who guide along the ecotones or margins where two or more constituencies, specialties or disciplines meet. Leading from this space between involves navigating the threshold between their own inner world of gifts, innate talents and vocation and the outer world of outcomes and action.

It means aligning their aspirations and calling with the innate life force for change and renewal, respecting paradox and differences, listening for multiple perspectives, and risking being authentic as an alternative to conforming to prescribed roles and responsibilities. This ability to reach beyond their own expertise to access the unique power of learning at the intersections of many disciplines distinguishes regenerative leaders at the vanguard of their fields.

We can hear the echo of this impulse in a young architectural graduate's reflections on what the University of Waterloo co-op program meant for him. When asked what gave him the courage to keep pushing to use the university as a hub for transforming and revitalizing the downtown core into a renaissance of shops and restaurants, he paraphrases "Why not?" — the current motto of the Waterloo Way.

"*Why not*," he said, "reflects the lively learning spirit of the place… a maverick, risky and playful attitude toward life. It also alludes to the importance of connections and recognizing windows of opportunity and anticipating what is to come. Furthermore, it is a story of hope and optimism and a love of home."

Embracing Beauty:

The Timeless Path to Place and Placemaking

We heard this same spirit of "Why not" in the optimistic words of the late Apple founder Steve Jobs when he said, "If we are going to make things in our lives, we might as well make them beautiful." (Issacson, 2011.)

Shortly after Jobs passed away, architect Michel Graves said, "He's been compared to Einstein and Edison, but he should really be compared to Picasso." Like other great artists, regenerative leaders don't always act incrementally. Sometimes they radically change the whole form they are working on. And what leads to this transformation is beauty. Power may inspire the mind of a leader, but it is beauty that inspires their soul. Power helps us get things done, but it is beauty that grips the imagination and inspires what needs to get done. Power may define what we think we need, but it is beauty that inspires and helps us find promise in an uncertain world.

For Jobs, being dedicated to creating beauty transformed his business. It was the defining emotion that guided the edifice of the business and all of its strategic thinking. Jobs was one of the first to incorporate a level of aesthetics in Apple products that had not been part of the computer world before. While he was an accomplished business strategist, he was first and foremost a craftsman and an artist.

"I want tactile experience to set the tone," Jobs said. Biographer Walter Issacson notes in his book *Steve Jobs*, "And what lay at the heart of the experience of touch for Jobs was delight." From his earliest days at Apple, Jobs was obsessed with delighting the customer with the joyful use of the product itself.

He loved finely designed and crafted things like Ansel Adams's prints and Bösendorfer pianos. He displayed a Bösendorfer handcrafted grand piano in the main foyer of the Apple offices to serve as a daily reminder that Apple employees were not only engineers but designers and craftspeople. Jobs wanted them to see their work as art and to carry this aesthetic throughout all phases of the design and manufacturing process.

Jobs envisioned marrying together arts and great design that expressed the elegance of human touch — even romance. What was most important for him was not making money but putting the quest for beauty back into the mainstream of human consciousness.

The ease of use, the simplicity of design, the flow of operation — all these and more lay at the heart of Jobs' vision for creating not only functional but artful innovation. This went beyond asking what the customer wanted, because the customer themselves may not have thought this was possible. In place of focus groups, benchmarking and market surveys, his approach was to surprise the customer with innovations they could not have dreamed possible.

Communicating through touch invites empathy with the other. It enables us to connect with the felt sense of the experience itself. The simplicity of design, the ease, flow and intuitive logic of operations, the tactile pleasure and delight of the touch screen, invite us into the natural and intuitive flow of experience with the confidence that each element is true to itself and couldn't be more or less than what it is. This iterative movement of going over it time and time again in order to reduce complicated steps to their most essential and simplest form is at the core of the art of innovation.

Poet and author John O'Donahue in his 2004 book *On Beauty* writes, "The time is right for the artistic imagination of each of us to co-create the leadership that the world most needs and deserves."

If Level 1 tactical leadership focuses on action, practicality and control, and Level 2 strategic leadership focuses on knowledge, planning and prediction, then Level 3 regenerative leadership focuses on transforming our world through the aesthetics of beauty, touch, possibility and the soul of place.

With regard to this soulful aspect of leadership, O'Donahue says, "Twenty-first-century society yearns for a leadership of possibility, a leadership based more on hope, aspiration, innovation and beauty than on the replication of historical patterns of contained pragmatism."

What would it take to embrace beauty, artistry and placemaking as practices for illuminating our path to an uncertain future? As we undergo a fundamental realignment from an industrial and knowledge-based mindset to the biological age, we will witness a resurgence in the work of craft as a vocation and practice — a leadership practice in which the revival of invention and design that are specific to place will once again serve as a central building block for creating the soul of a new economy. The quest for beauty is the bridge that brings leadership and work of craft together again.

SEEING THE WORLD GRATEFULLY:

RECLAIMING THE ART OF MAKING THINGS

When we find ourselves on uncharted terrain, it may be less important to know where we are going than to understand where we've been and where we are now.

– Pat Thompson

While we have mastered the art of thinking, many have lost the art of making things. A colleague, writer and consultant Pat Thompson, in her 2011 essay "The Dark Horse Conversation," opens the door to creating beauty through the art of making, pointing us toward a leadership renaissance in the following story:

> In 2010, I was called on by YMCA Canada to help its new chief executive officer engage member associations in renewing the national federation. My role was to support them in telling the new story that would guide their collaboration.
>
> Much of what we did was planned and predictable but not everything.

An idea for a special project landed in the middle of an ambitious workload and string of deadlines... The decision was taken to build a table for Canada's YMCA—a ten-foot boardroom table made from wood and artifacts from every YMCA and YMCA-YWCA in the country; artifacts that tell stories about what defines and inspires their work.

We enlisted the Brothers Dressler to build it. Twins Jason and Lars are two gifted contemporary furniture craftsmen who have mastered the art of repurposing old materials. We also called on John Beebe for his skill with light and shadow to photograph and document many disparate pieces becoming one beautiful and useful piece of art.

One year later, the table was unveiled alongside a comprehensive federation strategic plan. Both creations carry the fingerprints of every YMCA and YMCA-YWCA and tell the story in dramatically different ways. The plan sent them off in a new direction, and the table calls them home again.

Re-engaging with the work of craft involves a revival of an ancient and time-honoured practice that has been pushed to the margins of our knowledge-and industrial-based economy. To find our way into a post-industrial world, we need to reconnect with our pre-industrial world and the ancient wisdom we've forfeited — a practice that can bring us home again.

This does not mean a complete return to some archaic or nostalgic moment from the medieval past. Rather, it is to assume a sense of reverence for a form of work — and an *attitude* to work — that goes beyond skill or efficiency to something more reverent and sacred. It speaks to dedicating ourselves to those unique gifts that connect us deeply to the soul of place and inspires a craftsperson-like desire to achieve our very best. In this respect, filling a space in a beautiful way is the connective tissue that unites the soul of craftwork and the soul of leadership as two eyes that share a common sight.

Steve Jobs devoted every moment of his time as a leader to thinking about beauty, design and place. He was as keenly interested in the design of Apple's new offices in Cupertino as he was in crafting the simplistic beauty and clarity of every product. He believed you could not innovate in a bubble. Everything is part of a larger pattern that is intimately connected to the other.

We don't need to be world-changers to be regenerative leaders. How often have we been in a busy restaurant and noticed there is one server who can take in the pattern and flow of the entire scene all in one glance? Even if they are not serving our table, they notice us and can attract the attention of our server in an instant.

This quality of mindfulness and attention to the energy, tone, flow and feeling of a place is the signature strength and characteristic of regenerative leaders. This is their craft and, as we will explore, they work with it in many ways.

Few of us have that now. Too often we feel we have lost our craft and find ourselves placeless and overwhelmed in a busy and fragmented world. We don't know what we love, where we come from or what we are called to do. Nor do we have anything that truly absorbs our heart and imagination. We long for work that is a life-absorbing process that connects us intimately with a sense of place and calling — of home. Most importantly, like the regenerative leaders I have briefly described, we each in our own way long to break free of the constraints of the day-to-day to pursue a dream and create a place from which to pursue what may appear to be impossible.

These yearnings reflect a world out of balance. As I have suggested, we are the inheritors of not one, but two great streams and rich traditions through all of human history — the *Homo sapiens* (the wise ones), who have mastered the science of the mind, and another, the *Homo faber* (the makers), who have mastered the wisdom of the heart and the intelligence of the hand.

While the method of scientific logos or the *Homo sapiens* is to understand things by reducing them to their parts, the aim of craft as mythos and the *Homo faber* is to put them back together again. By learning to see the world as whole, craft teaches us how to be with the mystery of the whole of existence, to be without the answer because there is no answer. In the words of John Keats, "to remain in uncertainties, mysteries, doubts without the irritable reaching after fact or reason" is the ultimate goal. In this ambiguous field the crafts-person finds a certain peace. It is comforting to know that when we venture outside the bright illumination of our known world we will have our craft, and in this world of vast uncertainties our craft will help us see.

Among the underpinnings of place I am exploring here, craftwork is perhaps the most mysterious and difficult to describe in words. Yet it is central to any exploration of place, because craft connects us with the intimacy of our surroundings and brings us home to our own sense of calling and vocation. Craftwork is, first and foremost, a conversation with *place*. It is like a second nervous system that trans-forms physical space into a generative space that welcomes beauty, mastery and the imaginative spirit. It does so through tapping into that sacred desire to manifest beauty and bring out the very best of things.

The German-American philosopher Hannah Arendt describes this ancient practice in the context of *Homo faber* being the architects, the builders, the designers, the artists and the placemakers. These are the ones who not only think about, but also create, our mythic world — a world that both stands in the spaces between the human community and unites them.

The root of intelligence itself is *intellegere*, which means to gather *in between*. This is the work of craft, and it represents the re-embodiment of experience as a cellular process of breathing, digesting, thinking, feeling and sensing. We often overlook the power of *Homo faber* to transform physical space and create generative fields for learning. It means discovering how to see the world differently. This act of appreciative perception — of taking in our world in a spirit of gratitude and delight — is at the heart of all forms of craftwork.

To see the world gratefully from the perspective of craft means, for example, shifting from a logical rational worldview to a more intuitive and sense-based one. It means rebalancing our tendency for romanticizing engineering and technology with revaluing nature and the organic. It means being more accepting of ambiguity and contradiction, and recognizing that the eternal cycles of creation — including the balance of light and the opaque — help us appreciate that to be on the descending arc is also important; we don't need to be in the full flower of creation all the time.

As a whole body-mind experience, craft brings our world back into balance and helps us understand what it means to be truly and fully human. While we associate craftwork more narrowly with objects and things, we overlook the larger calling to the work of craft, which is, first and foremost, a *conversation* with the place we are in.

CRAFT AS AN ATTITUDE:

OPENING TO A WONDERFUL OTHERNESS

In Pat Thompson's account of the creation of the YMCA table, the artifacts and materials used to build the table came specifically from the places and stories that defined and inspired the builders' work. This is the power of craftwork; it touches everyone who desires, in some fundamental way, to bring their aspirations alive through interacting with and contributing to the creation of something of quality in *any* field.

Most importantly, the work of craft reminds us that, as mythologist Walter Otto writes, "The creative phenomenon must be its own witness — the human mind cannot become creative by itself, even under the most favourable of circumstances, it needs to be touched and inspired by a wonderful otherness, and this forms the most important part of the creative process no matter how gifted we are thought to be." (Otto, 1969.)

And this is central to the mindset of the craftsperson, which is to shift the focus to the value you bring to the other rather than to the value the work brings to you. In craft, what you bring to the work is vital. It is an act of selflessness and generosity. It is also what makes our unique contribution possible.

So craft engages this wonderful otherness. It is this intertwining ourselves with another that generates the synaptic connections that enable the mind to learn and grow.

As such, the work of craft is a unifying force. Through the presence of another, including the materials and the environment, it helps us see the patterns of connection between the parts and helps us see our world as whole. In craftwork, mastery is not only in how we achieve the end result but also in how we can take two or more things that seem to have no connection and *blend* them together.

In craft, it is not only how we do the work but how we bring ourselves to the work that creates an emergent third thing in the space between that did not exist before. Being deeply engaged in the work of blending and emergence opens up this inner world of otherness in which new qualities of awareness arise.

Cultivating this craftsperson-like understanding of how to bring things alive extended well into the 19th century but became marginalized during both the industrial and technological ages. Despite the trend away from the development of these skills, in some domains, they have been carried forward.

In my own piano instruction, for example, I was taught to practise in a traditional craftwork way, which involved bringing myself to the work through developing proficiency based on foundational skills. Many hours and days were devoted to the mastery of fingering, hand positions, tempo, harmony and scales. And while many avoid this technical work because it feels like drudgery and they don't know what's in it for them, constant practice offers more than may meet the eye. Learning foundational skills gives one a base from which to execute more complex ideas later on.

Author Michael Sennet writes of this when he suggests that craft is not only a skill but an attitude toward a way of working that serves the computer programmer, the doctor, the artist and the parent

(Sennett, 2009). Everything improves when we see craft as learning to build proficiency in relationship to the other— including seeing the materials at hand as vibrant and alive — and not just working with inanimate objects or as a trained skill acquired through use.

Herbert Dreyfus in his 2011 book *All Things Shining* writes of this relational dimension of craft:

> The skilled surgeon sees something more than a broken and bloody leg; he sees a particular kind of break, one that requires this particular surgical technique to fix it. Likewise, we hear people say that the successful running back has 'great vision,' and the point guard has extraordinary 'court sense.'

This sensing of something other as alive and holding its own integrity in relation to yourself is the foundation of craft. When I am at the piano, I am playing more than notes and chords. I am absorbing the culture I am in — the atmosphere, the language, the feeling and the full surround — and I am expressing all of this in a musical form.

Doctors, lawyers, nurses and leaders (just like pianists, artists and potters) hold their work as craft when they realize that, while they may think their work is about results and the need to know, the reality is that it is about being in a state of inquiry and not knowing. When they think that craft is free of obligation, they realize that craft is about the obligation of integrating their work so that it connects with the larger whole. Or when they think work is about the desire for skills and certainty, they discover that in "craft time," failure and delay is a necessary part of creating.

The real risk in craft is not failure but the fear of failure. Attitude — the willingness to be always in the inquiry, the question, the forming, and the relationship where risk, surprise and failure are always a possibility — is everything in craft. It is being open to learning from what the moment is calling for. This may be even more central than talent or technique.

WHOLEHEARTEDNESS:

THE ATTUNEMENT OF HEART, MIND AND HAND

Craft is the expression of wholeheartedness. When the mind listens for the longings of the heart and the leadings of the hand, we come into a deeper attunement with the place we are in.

British Columbia artist Brent Comber, who is known as the "wood whisperer," speaks about being drawn to wood because of its connection to place. "Indigenous wood talks about climate, it talks about geography, it talks about permanence — all the things he says that he loves about the West Coast." (McGinn, 2013.)

The craftsperson is guided as much by the hand and the heart as they are by the mind. In order to be connected to the material and to the place, the guidance of the hand is essential to craftwork. This is the case whether the work of the hand is physical, as in craft skills, or symbolic, as in opening one's hands as a gesture of yes and seeing one's destiny unfold before them. With craft, we cannot anticipate or decide beforehand all that we want something to be. We have to live into what the work is yearning for and do so by giving in to where the intelligence of our hands leads. What leads the hand is not logic or reason but being attuned to the longings of the heart and the embodiment of desire.

As a pianist, there are three ways in which this sense of wholeheartedness guides my playing. First, meaningful distinctions can be made in the type of wood, construction, tuning, action, and sound of each note I play. Each piano is distinct and has its own personality. I need to begin with the desire to discover how this piano wants to be played — its sweet spot, and keys or sections of the instrument that are feel-good places where I can fully express myself or try to approach in a different way.

Second, each time I play, I am in a unique physical, emotional and mental place. When I fulfill my desire to be in the moment, my hands are more sensitized to the differences in the temperature, responsiveness and flexibility of the instrument. I cannot go on automatic and play by rote. Since I am in a different atmosphere each time, the music reflects this, and I cannot play the same way twice.

Third, there is an intimacy between the hand, the piano's keys and the wood that includes a desire to connect to the full surround. Each place is its own natural cathedral, even — and more particularly — the small and the intimate. So I play not only for myself but out of the inner desire for my hands to be the instrument through which the fullness of the life force flows from all that surrounds and envelops me.

Being the soundtrack for life's greater desire is the means through which I express the uniqueness of the place in which I find myself playing. This intimate connection to a place helps us listen deeply and express through our craft whatever that place is longing for. Places don't only speak to us; they speak through us. There is no other way for us to discover the roots of our own desire than through the instructions that come to us from the heart's longing in a place-based world.

Playing the piano, therefore, as with any craft that requires long hours of dedicated practice, is sacred work. And the larger surround in which it is brought into being is sacred ground. As I discovered in my childhood imagination, the piano itself is alive. Each side — the player and the piano — brings out what is best in the other. It is this sacred desire that brings me back to the piano time and time again.

If we discount the intelligence of the hand and keep our attention to just what is within our mind, which can be fearful of the unknown, we may default to some pre-existing and unconscious pattern of habit or routine. Too often, this finely tuned conversation between the ear, the mind, the heart and the hand that craft brings has been fragmented — reduced to a job where the output is measured by the part, the minute or the hour.

In *The Work of Craft*, Carla Needleman wrote, "If I am fearful, I will lead with my mind, and the mind, in the life study of a craft, needs to be passive, to be there, but to be passive to watch without putting an end to the process by summing up." (Needleman, 1993.)

But leading with the hand is not an easy feat in a world where our efforts to be smarter, more rational and more efficient are what are rewarded. The *Homo faber* in us has been allowed to atrophy. It takes a dedicated and committed heart to keep it alive.

We hear this sentiment expressed through the words of stone master Alan Bird when he says, "Listening to the ring of the stone is very important... the sweetness of the sound of that chisel as it cuts is all language to the mason, and he's reading that as it comes off. He has to know, as soon as he hears that little sound (of imperfection), that something is not quite right. That will make him check, stop, look at what's happening." (Bird, 1991.)

In a world striving for invariance — and where dominance and control over nature has been paramount — the stone master is something of an anachronism. How in our modern world do we explain or understand a form of work where we are always an apprentice to place and the only true master is the stone?

This sense of yielding control and following where our work is taking us — sensing where it wants to go — can create an impression of incompleteness and ambiguity. This dedication to the sense of quickening (Immanuel Kant, for example, referred to music as the "quickening art") of the work and, simultaneously, the sometimes-long, slow progress of craft, suggests that it is motivated more by a sense of yearning than achievement. In other words, craftwork is more than the work; it is the longing to be reunited with nature itself.

As we find ourselves in a world of unceasing change and disorder where leaders can no longer plan with certainty, craft serves as a powerful and ancient metaphor for reuniting the inner mythic life with the work of logos in the world.

As such, craft fills our heart's hunger for work that has meaning, a sense of place and the opportunity to participate in the service of a higher calling. We long to be part of a greater journey of pilgrimage, as well as apprentices to a discipline that adds value to the world so we can see our significance in the larger order of things.

VOCATIONAL RENEWAL:

RE-IMAGINING THE NATURE OF WORK

By sensing into the complexity of the whole of the system and seeing its diverse patterns and connections, regenerative leaders are geographers and mapmakers. They have the ability to take every situation they encounter and create meaning through crafting representational models that reflect how they think and feel about themselves and others. This internal model determines how and what they see, what emotional value they assign to things, and how good they are at predicting what may come next.

For some leaders that model may be military strategy; for others it may be competitive sports or technology. For regenerative leaders, a new model they may use to represent their reality comes either explicitly or implicitly from the work of craft.

Craftwork is neither whimsical nor abstract. It is the primary force of our natural vocation announcing itself.

Craft is regenerative. Where many resources in our community, including roads, buildings and programs, may be exhausted through use, artists are constantly renewed through their art form — and anything can be an art form. When they write a poem, they want to write another poem. When they write a book, they want to write another book. They love what they do, and they need to do what they love. Their work is a gift, and as a gift it needs to stay in circulation.

If this is true, what can we learn about regenerative leadership through the language and practice of craftwork? Let's look at the following possibilities.

Transforming Leadership, Transforming Ourselves

When we are transforming our world, we are also transforming ourselves.

In craftwork there often exists a feedback loop between the craftsperson and the craft. Just as the craftsperson is transforming the work, they themselves are being transformed by the work. We most commonly think of how the materials come alive in the craftsperson's hand, but it can also be true in other contexts as well. Regenerative leadership does not necessarily impose an order. As in the work of craft, it follows the trajectory of a project's own timing and unfolding, one that is natural and organic, making visible in its progress an invisible order that already exists — one that changes as the leaders themselves evolve.

Several years ago, a small group of us hosted four gatherings collectively named "Leading for Transformation" at Seasons at the conference centre of the Fetzer Institute. Seasons is tucked into the side of a hill near Kalamazoo, Michigan, and built of limestone and huge timbers, native Michigan materials. The vast window that opened out into the woods carried its own messages about the nature of things. In autumn and spring, through brilliant sunshine and surprise thunderstorms, we gathered in circles, large and small, to share stories and insights about transformation, leadership and change.

In another setting or time, we might have expected that these deliberations would have had a singularly academic framing. The invited participants would present their theories, and we would listen objectively and observe. But somehow the setting, the structure of the conversations, the tone setting of music, poetry and the fresh thinking and stories of so many who joined us grounded our experience and made them more like an informal retreat. As we listened, we also joined in; as the participants were being transformed by the experience, so were we, as the stewards of the process. (6)

In craftwork, as in leadership, knowing is the greatest obstacle to learning and certainty is the greatest obstacle to seeing. Each place calls out something unique in us, something that could not exist in any other time or place. To be willing to accept our vulnerability and not-knowing and to be touched by what we are seeing and hearing are the first steps in both transforming and being transformed by the work itself.

PURPOSEFULNESS: TAKING THE LONG VIEW

In craft, the work itself holds an inner design that carries the seed of its own unfolding.

In the work of craft, the craftsperson seeks to enter into the flow of life, to add something to the legacy of what has gone before. This means being involved in work that stands for something, work that lasts and may outlive the craftspeople themselves. To create anything in craft means taking this long view. If we rush into craft, we are liable to miss the whole thing. And while craftwork may sometimes appear random, chaotic and even wrong-headed from the outside, it is actually highly coherent, elegant, even compelling when experienced from within.

This is particularly true when we understand that the work itself has an inner design that carries the seed of its own potential. When we work within this design, the work naturally emerges. It is when we try to move ahead by force of will, or through pressure or urgency, that this internal order is disturbed and our progress impeded.

Poet William Stafford believed that to be connected to this natural order we need to stay in alignment with what is already unfolding. That is, to be careful to distinguish between what is occurring naturally and what we believe *ought* to be happening. When Stafford did this — asking what these fragments of thoughts, patterns and images were trying to say — poems came to him freely and abundantly. He thought of this as a thread and that as long as we were holding and following the thread, we could not get lost.

Stafford's words are reassuring. The image of the thread is a reminder that life knows what it is doing, that even in those darkest moments when we have no plan and can see no clear way forward, we have a thread. As long as we hold the thread a way will open before us.

For regenerative leaders, this means that instead of trying to impose their will based on what they believe ought to happen, they maintain a heightened state of attention for what is already vital and alive in the situation and unfolding naturally. Even when the future and the long view cannot be predicted, the deeper purposes of things may be imagined and felt. Rather than try to avoid surprise, leaders can see their work as a form of craft that invites surprise, embraces uncertainty and instructs us in how to be open to and learn from the unexpected and to engage a larger unknown.

The work of craft does not unfold in isolation from our colleagues, our community or our history. It is always being created in relationship to the place in which it unfolds. Craft is connected to a trajectory that may have started long before our time and may continue long after. When time is not the primary driver, craft invites a sense of neutrality, patience and compassion. In place of immediate results, the craftsperson assumes the obligation to carry forward a purpose, perhaps first articulated by others and then passed along through them to be handed over to those who follow.

In this sense, the craftsperson is always the apprentice. The material at hand, whether it is the clay, the musical instrument, the stretched canvas, the blank page, the strategic plan or a sense of one's own leadership and destiny, awakens in the work a sense of humility as we realize it may take ages to perfect or realize. Even as this choice to take the time is being made, the craftsperson knows that, when all is done, other forces are also at play, and no one really perfects it all on their own.

COLLABORATION: BONDING WITH THE OTHER

A major impediment to workplace success is the quality of the environment and culture in which most people work. In a healthy environment, leaders are not trained; they emerge naturally out of the quality of the place and culture itself.

Seeing our work, whatever it may be, as craft tunes us to relationship. It is a relationship that grows and deepens over time. Creating places for exploring what we do not yet know, spaces where we can be present to what is unformed and incomplete, sets in motion a process of bonding with the other. Bonding, developing a sense of empathic resonance with the other, is the natural result of working with materials or aspirations we do not completely control.

As such, the work of craft opens a third space between the craftsperson and the work, a space between self and other, that holds a subtle power and informs and guides the formation of the work itself even more than the will of the craftsperson. Reading the stone, the fall of the brush on the canvas, the weight of the hand as it sinks into the piano key, serving a new client — all of these are sources of complex information for the sensing body of the craftperson to make meaning of.

The process of listening into the unfolding of the work and asking what it wants from us suggests how the work of craft itself speaks to us. Whether it is playing an instrument, firing a pot in the kiln or interacting with another, the work of craft enters into and is informed through the body's inner wisdom regarding what is needed. It is this process of body-mind integration that accounts for the deep collaborative bonding of craft.

When we see work as craft, we create a space for the complex ecology of the work environment to unfold. In a healthy environment, leaders do not need to be trained; they emerge naturally out of the nourishment of the work culture itself.

FAITHFULNESS: THE ART OF MINIMUM FORCE

What matters most in craft is the thing we cannot explain.

Mahatma Ghandi once said that working with the hands is the apprenticeship of honesty. The hands don't lie. We may rationalize how and what we think, but not what we touch and feel. Working and creating with our hands offers a kind of rhythm with life. By listening, touching, sensing, releasing and letting go, we become more and more attuned to the intimate exchange between our hand, our heart and our mind.

This ease of connection in craft brings to mind the words of French painter Georges Braque: "Art happens." When we reflect on craft, only one thing counts: the thing you can't explain. In the busyness of our days, we often forget this mystery. We get caught up in what seems an overworked and over-processed world where what feeds us does not fill us. We hunger for what is real and authentic — words, ideas, connections and possibilities, ideas that come out of the earth with the roots and dirt on them.

Acknowledging this mystery in how art happens, regenerative leaders often pilot not from out front but from behind. They know they do not have all the answers and find faith in the realization that leading from out front is often akin to leading by flashlight or using a laser in a darkened room. Our certainties blind us to hidden opportunities. These only come to light with the illumination of the candle, whose opaque light brings the darkened corners into view.

Thus the question in craft is, how do we keep the flame of the candle alive? What is already present that we are not seeing? And what does it mean to create safe places where we can build trust and goodwill to influence outcomes we cannot directly control?

TRUST: CREATING THE PATH AS WE WALK

Wanderer, there is no path. You lay the path by walking.

– Antonio Machado

Unlike the stable markets in years past, when you could rely on tools, skills and answers, we are entering a time when we will need to shape conversations around the questions that really matter in order to find our path into the future and a larger unknown.

A path, unlike a road, does not move directly from point A to point B. Instead it adapts to the natural contours of the place in which it finds itself. As ecologist Wendell Berry writes, "A road... embodies a resistance against the landscape. Its reason is not simply the necessity for movement, but haste. It wishes us to avoid contact with the landscape, it seeks so far as possible to go over the country rather than through it." (Berry, 1981.)

Those who embraced an Industrial Age mindset were road-builders. Their focus was not on accommodating place but overcoming it — to progress with the least effort by removing all obstacles in their way. If the Industrial Age mindset was to be road-builders, leading to the destruction of landscape, the craftsperson's mindset is to be path-makers who seek to restore and make amends with the landscape.

Berry writes, "A path is more than a habit that comes with knowledge of a place. It is a sort of ritual of familiarity… a form of contact with a known landscape." (Ibid, 1981.)

By seeing our places not as alien to our interests but as home for our craft, we restore the sanctity of wild landscapes again. By holding a respectful relationship with the land, including the harmonious play of light and shadow, the rustling of the wind through the pine tree, the call of a wood thrush, the nurturing of community, we can imagine being an intimate part of nature's symmetries and rearrange our life according to this same order.

REST: DISCOVERING WHAT NOURISHES US

Feeling is the emergent intelligence of connectivity. Our feelings put things together that we cannot see in other ways. But to feel, we also need to be rested — and to be still.

All work is half rest. Nature cannot thrive in full flower all the time. Neither can we. "What is enough?" we ask. In a world that holds that enough is never enough, we will not grant our soul the time it needs to empty, to digest, to assimilate and to be still.

Dormancy, decay and regeneration are as much a part of the life force as are growth and flowering. The absence of this deep time of gestation can lead to confusion and erosion of the force of life itself. Wayne Muller, in his book *Sabbath* (Muller, 2000), reminds us that what may seem to be a successful life can also be a violent one. A successful life is often seen as a busy, time-bound life in which so much of our sense of place and relationships is compromised in our rush to meet some pressing goal.

Plants can only grow as high as they grow deep. To reach for and achieve our highest aspirations, we must also live a deeply rooted life. To do otherwise is to be at the mercy of the turbulence of the larger world. We can only withstand the stronger forces on the outside if we are deeply rooted to the subtle forces within ourselves. Our sense of duty and responsibility often overrides our intuition and good judgment. It becomes difficult to settle, to find a place of rest from which to grow. Yet, as Muller suggests, the world aches for just that — the generosity of well-rested people.

Rest offers the gift of time and space in which we can consider what it is that brings us back to the work. For many, it is to discover and create life — to follow the thread that brings meaning and significance to days that may feel meaningless otherwise. Ultimately, what lies behind this quest is the even deeper longing to connect with that which nourishes us.

To follow what nourishes us is not always easy. It can be frightening, because it means letting go of one's priorities or plans in such a way that we create *only* from what truly moves and inspires us. In a world where we have been taught to set aside our own preferences to meet the needs of others, this appears to be the most selfish of acts. And yet we cannot truly serve others if we have not yet first discovered what holds meaning for us.

This form of service begins with creating a language of place that is a living and authentic expression of what we truly and honestly like. To listen, to pause, to feel, to look, to taste, to ask "What feels right here?" Our technology sometimes flattens our relationship to language. We forget that language is not only a resource that is instrumental in getting things done but also an instrument for creating transformative shifts in consciousness that change what we hear, what we see and how we think. As my colleague, poet and educator Judy Brown, wrote, "The capacity of people to remain centered and steady in the midst of uncertainty, surprise and new possibilities often rides on the power of the language that we choose to express the circumstances in which we find ourselves." (Banff Forum, 2010.)

We will not create ugliness and utility if we offer the world only that which truly nourishes us. This is because what nourishes us is not an act of the mind but of the heart. The heart is made even more generous by those experiences that instill a sense of affection, reverence and home.

THE POWER OF ITERATION:
FOLLOWING WHAT THE WORK WANTS TO BE

Working iteratively holds a sense of ease — even as it appears difficult from the outside.

As a pianist and composer, I go over a composition time and time again, listening and feeling for the underlying pattern and all the different ways a piece of music may go. I make a lot of mistakes and go down blind alleys as I explore the emerging composition's changing directions. Fuzziness and ambiguity are characteristic of any regenerative process and create openings for what needs to occur. To keep that openness, it is always best to seek approximations rather than precision. By taking incremental steps, we have the liberty to create and adjust as we go.

Any iterative process is nurtured more by curiosity than correctness. A healthy curiosity means giving way to the experience itself so that we may enter the flow of our own felt life with our tools, materials and knowledge, not only to speak through them but to let them speak through us.

When we push for results rather than let the materials speak, the desire for success and positive outcomes impedes this flow. This also happens when we are driven by a construct in our mind rather than by what is organically forming in the work itself. This constricts the work of craft, dulls our senses and limits the chance of bringing something of ourselves — something truly unique and original — into the world.

Each iteration contributes to enhancing and refining the imagination so that we are able to make better aesthetic choices later on. In this context, to be iterative is not to correct errors or mistakes but to engage them so as to be more aligned with a process of emergence that lies beneath. Working in this way holds within it a sense of naturalness and simplicity even when it may appear difficult and complex to someone observing it from the outside.

Letting Go: Assuming a Lightness of Being

That which is creative must create itself. It is energy without a reason, a force that creates out of its own accord.

– John Keats Musicians sometimes set aside their well-known repertoires to be open to the mystery of the moment and where it may want to go. In craft, the process itself *is* the content, and it is often difficult to explain where ideas come from and where they may lead.

As with any process that builds upon itself, it cannot be preconceived or created fully in anticipation or out of a concept formed in advance. This includes letting go of old forms in order to open a space and make a home for new forms to come in. This willingness to be in the mystery, to create something from nothing, to stand on the cusp between the past, the present and the future, to trust one's own experience and inner knowing, no matter how paradoxical it may seem, lies at the heart of craft. The unity of the mind, the heart and the hand is always fragile because it is always being tested.

For example, on the one hand, craftwork accepts the age-old nature of craft including the slowness, patience, and deliberation of history and "craft time." Craftspeople also appreciate how the dedication to craft reaches toward the future, which signals the need to seize the moment with alertness, engagement and acceptance of risk.

By following the lead of the hand, the craftsperson learns the fine art of dropping fully into each moment and *at the same time* risking the release and letting go into the next. The work of craft acknowledges this contradiction and assumes a lightness of being so that the hands touch the moment and also reach out and risk the future by touching the next moment. This is a profound act of trust because, even as the craftsperson makes this leap of faith, carried forward by this intuitive surge of energy, a force that seems to act without a reason, they cannot say with certainty what this next moment will bring.

The Art of the Impossible:
The Inner Necessity of Craftwork

So much of what we create comes from a source unknown to us.

If craft is hard, it is so because it is teaching us these lessons. We do craftwork not because it is possible but because it is necessary. And, because it is necessary, craftwork sets us on the path toward inner grace as we come to realize that we are not only shaping the work; we are also shaping ourselves.

This is what brings us back time and time again. There is an inner necessity to craftwork that is also its grace. We create what we create because we cannot do anything else.

This complete absorption in the work helps us realize that so much of what we create, in whatever we are doing — in leadership, teaching, living or work — comes from a place unknown to us. It is natural to feel uncertain, because the insights we need to proceed are not always visible to the rational mind. To discover them, we must trust our own innate sense of aliveness. Our aliveness comes when we accept a certain humility with regard to what we know and can control and what we cannot.

This may also be the key to engaging the art of the impossible: to be open not only to what we know but to the aliveness of what we feel. In the same vein, we may ask ourselves what calls us to the work of craft in the first place. Often what calls out to us is a voice that says, "I am doing this not because it is possible, but because it is necessary... *this* is what I came for... *this* is what I was born to do."

When we engage the art of the impossible, we draw our authority not only from an established body of content and expertise stored in memory but from a living process of thinking and feeling in the moment, feelings that include our doubts, perplexities, aspirations and fears. The exhilaration and fear we experience is normal; it's a natural response to the realization that we are creating not from our own will alone but from a deeply intuitive process in which new insights emerge afresh in our speaking, leading, teaching and playing *as we need it* from a source unknown to us — and not a moment before. We cannot master the art of the impossible without, at the same time, accepting this risk.

Acclaimed pianist Keith Jarrett, reflecting on an improvisational concert in Rio de Janeiro, said in a NPR interview with Guy Raz, "It's never the same... I have no idea, moment to moment, how to prepare for these things, either. What actually happens is so much in the moment, so much of a nanosecond. And I know a lot of people probably are skeptical about whether they really are always improvised. I myself even feel skeptical though I know they were."

This is the challenge for everyone and also the ultimate gift of craft-work. With the great uncertainties that lie before us, we need to dig deep for a fresh response. This includes the willingness to act even when we don't know what our actions may be.

The demands we see ahead do seem impossible. Perhaps improvising at the piano is impossible; speaking out of the moment is impossible; facilitating a large group dialogue is impossible; building trust in a team or an organization in turbulent times is impossible.

If we perform in a way that relies solely on the script of notes and chords and how things have gone before then, yes, these things are impossible to do. But if we attend to the circumstances at hand and sense into what we are uniquely being called to do in this place, we will be provided for and access what would otherwise be impossible to know or do.

This way of being with tasks — the sense that things work by their own schedule and that some invisible hand is also at work — is what helps us realize what we first believed was impossible to achieve.

An Architecture of Happiness:

Designing for the Beauty of the Human Spirit

It is in our nature to seek experiences that elevate the beauty of the human spirit through the design of places that generate feelings of happiness, hope, well-being and good will.

The intrinsic desire to fill a space in a beautiful way carries over into how we craft larger and more complex physical and natural environments so that they may also offer happiness, hope, good will and positive future. At this moment, people everywhere are looking for ways to heal the environments in which we live and work — environments that serve as a focal point for the natural expression of who we are and how our energy is naturally expressed.

This leads us to ask how we may engage in social experiments that build economies that honour local culture and heritage, celebrate the beauty of place and the human spirit, protect the environment, increase the resilience of local people and provide communities with the means to invest in the future and local design.

In *Artful Leadership* (2006), I write about how difficult it is to feel that we belong to something when there is nothing to belong to. It is as if we are engaged in the relentless and unforgiving creation of sameness. Leaders find no reprieve in their offices and cubicles. Humans are in truth fragile beings. When we design environments with no real sense of beauty, story or place, the human soul is lost in what James Howard Kunstler describes as a Geography of Nowhere (Kunstler, 1994). It is a geography in which everything looks the same and there is no sense of place any longer.

When we acknowledge our essential fragility, perhaps we can also recognize that everyone benefits from being in an environment where there is a sense of clarity, harmony and well-being. Isolation and loneliness are the epidemics of our time. Together they place a burden on the human psyche that is almost impossible to heal.

According to architect and designer Christopher Alexander, when we consider the design of our built environments, something as ephemeral as soul needs to serve as the underlying foundation for what we create. When we take the soul of a place into account, two things will stand out in our thinking.

First, the land itself, including its uniqueness, its history and story, will provide the context for what is built on it.

Second, the shape of buildings will not only be engineered but erected through "works of craft made by human hands so that the entire structure is a work of art."

With these two principles as a guide, we can step back and ask, in each moment, whether what we are designing possesses more or less soul and more or less presence, aliveness and nourishment as we move from one stage to the next.

Alexander amplifies this perspective toward the work of craft as a public practice. "For a creation to possess soul it tends to communicate a world view that has life, well-being, harmony, beauty, care and a sense of being whole. That is, it needs to have a feeling of freshness and generativity as if it could go on forever without running out of ideas." (Alexander, 2012.)

When everything is planned in advance and where there is no art or relationship with the environment, buildings are imposed on the land, not created out of it; therefore they cannot speak to, or appeal to, the feeling part of our own nature.

And buildings (or fine pianos or other great works created with care) are not finished when they are complete; they complete themselves through an intimate reciprocity with the user. Works of craft are not commodities but gifts. They cannot be perfected in advance but only through use.

For the past 20 years I have been playing and composing on a seven-foot Bösendorfer handcrafted piano from Vienna. I was disappointed when I first brought the piano into my home. It did not sound or feel like the Bösendorfers I had played on stage. The piano technician reassured me, however, and said that the piano was still not *complete.*

As time passed he suggested it would mould itself to my touch. And it did. Each year I discover new tonalities, overtones and thematic possibilities in the instrument — musical ideas I could not have imagined beforehand. The complex interaction of wood, tone and strings are a living architecture that evolves as the instrument and I become more fully ourselves each time I play. Now the Bösendorfer knows my voice so intimately I feel it is playing itself.

To design in a way that creates this living architecture is an act of trust and reciprocity. It involves being attentive to feedback and adaptation; all elements are perfected, the buildings telling a story and holding to a point of view, as they grow and expand over time.

In this context a recent article in *The New York Times* (Carey and Martin, October 2012) is relevant.

> In 2006 a 26-year-old architecture student, Michael Murphy, approached the global health pioneer Paul

Farmer after a lecture at Harvard. Mr. Murphy asked which architects Dr. Farmer had worked with to build the clinics, housing, schools and even the roads he had described in his talk. An aspiring social entrepreneur, Mr. Murphy was hoping to put his design degree to use by apprenticing with the humanitarian architects aiding Dr. Farmer's work. But it turns out, those architects didn't exist.

"I drew the last clinic on a napkin," Dr. Farmer told Mr. Murphy.

Soon after, Mr. Murphy flew to Rwanda, where he and a few other students, including Alan Ricks and Marika Shioiri-Clark, became Dr. Farmer's architects. Mr. Murphy lived in the country for over a year while the Butaro Hospital, which laborers built with local materials, was designed...

The Butaro Hospital is a breathtaking building with intricate lava rock walls made of stones cut by Rwandan masons, and it is full of brightly colored accent walls and breezeways bathed in light and air. Deep-green flora blossom everywhere. For the 340,000 people who live in this region of Northern Rwanda, the project marks a literal reclamation: an area that was once a site of genocidal violence is now a center for state-of-the-art medical care. Healing happens there. An unmistakable grace permeates the place.

This story points toward a possible future where regenerative leadership ultimately leads to the regeneration of public spaces. The goal is not just to build buildings and pave over parking lots but to "design our way to a more beautiful and just world." (Ibid, 2012.)

I had the opportunity to meet Mariko Shioriri-Clark at the Global Gathering of the Fetzer Institute in Assisi, Italy, in the fall of 2012. I was there to learn firsthand about the working principles of public-interest design an architecture of hope is based on.

Assisi itself is designated as a regional centre committed to exploring the intersection between nature, art and dialogue. It carries within its walls a spirit of contemplation, transformation and renewal. This may be the spirit of welcome and hospitality we consider introducing into many of our other public spaces.

In this context, when we think of public design in the future, there may be several principles to consider.

First and foremost is to bring about the transformation of any and all places and spaces — hospitals, parks, streetscapes, offices, libraries — through dialogue. Through working collaboratively we can bring to the surface our own thinking and preferences about spaces and places and how they work. We can also think together about how we imagine the nature of our shared common places. The purpose of these conversations is to acknowledge that everyone deserves good design and that everyone deserves to live in a world of dignity in which their deepest needs, desires and stories may be heard and respected.

Secondly, what if we lived in a world in which designers — and that includes all of us who carry a passion for beauty and functionality — were trained to listen, to observe and to improve the way things look and feel? We would soon see that all of us could be craftspeople dedicated to improving products, places and processes that are in desperate need of good design.

In this way, we may begin to reach the overwhelming majority of the world who don't benefit from product design but whose lifestyle and workplace are affected by the design of homes, workplaces and communities. We can engage in design that appeals to us as citizens and not only as consumers.

This approach to design would focus on using local materials and edifying local places and stories in order to design buildings and public spaces that both delight and heal. These are buildings that have ample natural light, open spaces and wide corridors diffusing the separation between the inside and outside environment.

According to the *New York Times* article, Michael Murphy realized "the developed world has much to learn about good, human-centered design from the developing world. After finishing the Butaro Hospital and returning to the United States, he was struck 'at how over-designed most hospitals are here — there's little natural airflow, a lack of color and craftsmanship, and few outdoor spaces to take a deep breath and gain some perspective.'" (Ibid, 2012.)

Thirdly, what if we created enlivening and dignified places in which to live and work through the introduction of natural systems and local materials that promote health, happiness and a sense of well-being? They are spaces that allow for natural and spontaneous interaction, walkability and invite opportunities for engagement and collaboration. They are places that represent a culture shift from design as exclusive and controlled by professionals to design in dialogue with and for the public interest — design that makes 'radical listening' a hallmark of its practice and thereby is a process, empowering and catalyzing social change by inviting everyone to think like a designer.

It catalyzes this change not by focusing on power and bartering across interest groups but on beauty, innovation, inclusivity and love as key factors in the design process. Every expression of good design is essentially an expression of love and dignity because it is based on a sense of service and generosity in which everyone is invited to contribute to enlivening and dignifying the design process.

In this context the design process is itself catalytic. It brings about change because it emerges from the community. The designer is like an anthropologist who listens to what the community wants from its public spaces. As such, design literacy is rooted not only in academic or design-school environments but in living environments, neighbourhoods and communities — any place where the integration of our mythic life is common to all and where the integration of art and beauty and functionality serve as our 'schools for life.'

In other words, the points of reference for dignified design are not lines and graphs on a page, but people, places, and neighbourhoods. An architecture of hope is an architecture of local conditions, ways and means. It is a world in which the purpose of design and craft is not to build up the creator but to create a world that is life-enhancing and where people can be emotionally nourished through an emphasis on space, subtlety, grace and adaptation. These serve as the foundation for enlivening the parts so they fit into a larger whole.

This idea of design as an embodiment of a dialogue between client and designer came naturally to architect Samuel Mockbee, one of the early practitioners of participatory place-based design. In his 1998 essay *"Architectural Design: The Everyday and Architecture"* he wrote, "The professional challenge... is how to avoid being so stunned by the power of modern technology and economic affluence that one does not lose sight of the fact that people and place matter... For me these small projects have in them the architectural essence to enchant us, to inspire us and ultimately to elevate our profession... They remind us that we can be as awed by the simple as by the complex and that if we pay attention, this will offer us a glimpse into what is essential to the future of American Architecture: its honesty." (Sinclair and Stohr, 2006.)

LIVING THE GIFT:

NURTURING AN ECONOMY OF GENEROSITY

A gift is not a gift until it is given.

– Lewis Hyde

The work of craft is the embodiment of the gift. That is, the gift is not a skill but an endowment given over for our use so long as we labour in its service, and for the betterment of others and not only ourselves.

It is also the nature of the gift to transcend what we believe is possible so that our destiny can be fulfilled. That is, our gifts bring us into a world of people, places, connections and synchronicities we would not have known otherwise.

The call to craft invites us to nurture the gifts that are latent in us today in order to build a world for tomorrow. This work cannot be achieved on our own. It is the community that sees the gift in us, and so it is in community that our gifts are woven together. It is in community that our gifts are offered as we create in the service of meeting the needs of another.

Connecting with and acting in the service of our gift is such a fundamental human need that social upheavals are often motivated not by financial poverty but the poverty of the imagination that arises when our gifts are not seen or wanted by others.

Historically, we've lived and thrived in economies of generosity, in which the primary mode of exchange was through our gifts. This may lead us to wonder what our economic system might look like if we rewarded not only productivity but generosity as well.

So when we think of buildings, communities and craft in the context of beauty, soul and aliveness, it is to imagine that, even though these may be dismissed as secondary values in the larger culture, they are essential values in a world enriched through acts of generosity and the exchange of gifts.

To be at home in the world is to be in a place where there is a fit between our gifts and the work we do in the world. This fit between our gift and our work will become the leading source of wealth creation in the future because the gift itself is regenerative. Where many of the resources in our current economy are de-generative because they deplete over time, the gift grows and expands through use.

How the gift does this is largely a mystery. As philosopher Martin Heidegger says, "More is given to us than is made by us." Without engineering it or even understanding how it works, the gift keeps giving. Since the gift is beyond our capacity to control or master, what is asked of us in return is to adopt an attitude of humility and generosity so that the full bounty of the gift can live through us and energize a more enchanted and more human world.

But for the world to progress, the gift needs to be kept in circulation. And for the gift to truly circulate, it needs to involve more than a transaction between two people. Gifts move in circles — they need at least a third person so that we establish a community of participation within which something greater than ourselves can evolve.

A Second Renaissance:

Crafting a World where Life Can Thrive

The constant search for being more whole and more alive is
the alchemy for creating a world where life can thrive.

We are at the threshold of crafting a new story — a story that holds
a vision for a shift of mind from focusing on preserving what we
have left to a world where we generate new life out of the seeds and
soil available to us.

The leaders who will thrive in the next century are those who realize
we are moving from an industrial model that is reductionist and narrowly disciplined to a biological model in which leaders are artists
and craftspeople who are comfortable with uncertainty, surprise and
constant change. It represents a movement toward seeing our environment as a garden — a dynamic, living ecosystem — in which
learning and adaptation are natural parts of our ongoing evolution.

Leaders in this second renaissance will be both curators and placemakers. As curators they will excel at helping others make sense
and craft choices out of the complexity of information available to
them. As place makers they will also be recognized for their ability

to design and create learning experiences so that others can learn and grow.

We may see the following occur as this leadership renaissance unfolds:

THINKING AHEAD IN DECADES

Leaders will think not in quarters or even years, but in decades. What will sustain them is having their actions rooted in some compelling and overarching aspiration — something they feel uniquely called to do that cannot be finished in their own lifetime but will be a legacy for others to complete. They will transform their unique gifts into services, processes and products crafted in micro or personal factories (like a garage next door), creating local and global ecologies of innovation.

ADOPTING ENABLING METAPHORS

Leaders will be legacy builders who, like symphony conductors, recognize leadership as a mysterious art in which they are 'shaping the invisible' in order to manifest a new possibility. Creating something out of nothing will be a new metaphor, and drawing from the language of different disciplines of practice including the arts, sciences and humanities will lead them to think outside the building and across the boundaries of different sectors and disciplines.

BECOMING THE NEW ARTISANS

Regenerative leaders will be our new artisans who define art to include anyone who is dedicated to bringing something of unique value that expresses their gifts and talents in whatever they do. They will be like their medieval or ancient predecessors who often developed their craft outside the castle or the formal walls of institutional life. In these older forms of craft there was often a heartfelt connection between the maker and the product as they strived for each piece to fit perfectly with the other. In this we see a renewal of the ancient commitment to creating whole cloth out of the ancient and organic interdependence of the parts. This attitude is very different from the planned and rigidly systematic and universal repetitive production of the parts that replaced the work of craft in the industrial age.

BUILDING FUTURES THROUGH COLLABORATION

These leaders will guide a new renaissance through enterprises that are more ecological, more local and more holistic and global in their thinking. They recognize long-term success is not in the branches of the tree in terms of its financial wealth or strategy but in the connectivity of the root structures where they can engage in conversations around complex questions of meaning, beauty and purpose. The interdependence of these collaborations are where they will engage intensely to create outcomes much better than what could have been conceived and created alone. This new ground of engagement will offer new and unexpected insights for adapting quickly to new situations. They will also serve as enablers who can connect islands of opportunity with others and bring people in from their obvious sphere of engagement to interact with other disciplines.

ENGAGING THE ART OF EMERGENCE

Guiding the new leaders' actions will be not only goals, plans or outcomes but access to the vast, invisible potential of knowing and being where the 'now' is. They will nurture a contemplative or reflective frame of mind wherein insights and awareness outside of our common ways of thinking can bubble up. This represents an important new dimension of work: to improvise and try something that has not been thought out in detail, something that cannot thrive in an environment dominated by objectives and outcomes. We are better at filling space than emptying it, but it may be by emptying our workspace that we make room to fulfill new possibilities. In so doing, they create safe places, protective boundaries and time for agile engagement so that small pieces can be cobbled together into a bigger picture.

MAKING BEAUTY NECESSARY

These leaders' primary focus will not be on metrics, compensation or information but on what is life-affirming through refocusing on aesthetics, beauty, harmony and the sensory experience — on creating products, processes, services and craft through a focus on design, touch and feel. They will be drawn to creating beautiful and authentic work out of raw forms and disorganized materials. They will be looking for the qualities and essences of things in products and relationships. And they will do so by discriminating between what is required and what is enlivening.

BEING COMMITTED TO A PURPOSE AND VOCATION

Leaders will be rooted to what they are most committed to or called to do. They will see what they do more as a vocation than as work — a call to service in the fulfillment of an end larger than themselves. Salaries, benefits and other forms of compensation are, therefore, weak substitutes for being at home in whatever it is they do. They will recognize the new currency of legacy, values, culture, history and destiny and how these help define the larger story they wish to belong to. They will lead a surge toward the upswelling of movements and social action that furthers the well-being of public places and the quality of the common good. In so doing, they will create 'eco-system platforms' that have room for generating many seeds of ideas along with fertile soil for these seeds to take root and grow.

MICHAEL JONES

FROM CONSUMER TO CITIZEN

Leaders will ask "Why?" and "What if?" more than "How?" and "How much?" They will recognize that the places of the future will be co-created and will make their investments not only in projects and plans but also in building citizenship through investing in communities, relationships and places. Their interest will be in finding cracks and openings in the spaces between sectors and disciplines as found in neighbourhoods, associations and informal networks, and in crafting temporary but committed work teams and common places to gather together.

ENGAGING PRODUCTIVE AMBIGUITY

Leaders will be masters of big-picture thinking and productive ambiguity. They will come to appreciate that we often strive to make things explicit even though forcing things to become explicit changes their nature; it tends to make them mechanical and lifeless because we are trying to recreate what we already know. Productive ambiguity engages and finds strength in our vulnerability. This willingness to be vulnerable helps us move beyond the security of what is already known to what is not yet known.

VALUING LEADERSHIP FROM THE INSIDE OUT

Leaders will recognize that the most important question is not *how* you lead but *where* you lead from. This is the next frontier in leadership practice: leaders willing to be reflective and open-minded in ways that awaken them to their own inner nature and guide them toward the fulfillment of their aspirations and dreams. Leaders need to be leaders to themselves first. It is only then that people will follow them.

PART FOUR

GATHERING TOGETHER:

The Cultural Landscapes of Place

One of the legacies of the information age has been to flatten many aspects of collective human feeling and experience. As a result, we find ourselves in a world out of balance. We long for places to gather together and be swept up by a collective human emotion that awakens us to experiences of tolerance, openness, diversity and care. No outer teaching will affect human progress as much as our common interest in learning from one another. It is now a time for us to draw from the deep pool of our collective creative energy to craft a future to which we can all belong.

Every Voice Matters:

Creating Neighbourhoods in the Workplace

A colleague said recently, "Maybe we should change the name 'departments' in our workplaces to 'neighbourhoods.' This would reframe how we meet, talk and care for one another. When we think of departments as neighbourhoods, we would not meet — we would gather."

How can we create conversations that shift the leaders' focus from what they do in the world to who they *are* in the world — conversations that focus on changing our world views and not just on meeting the bottom line.

This is a time of expansion — a time when the cultural landscapes of place are bursting forth in new ways. However chaotic they may appear on the outside, these are times that have seen a surge of spontaneous engagement leading to a renewed sense of care for the community, the commons and the public square.

It was with this notion of creating a large conference that was not a meeting but a gathering in order to create a sense of their collective future together that a group of us had an exploratory meeting with Jaya Kumar, then president and CEO of Quaker Foods North America.

As Kumar said, "Too often the language we use reduces the scale of what we want to accomplish. As a result, we apply tactical solutions and expect transformational results. I want to engage our culture in a series of conversations around the theme 'Connecting for Our Future.' Conversations that can transform how we think and how we act."

The shared hope was that these conversations would encourage big-picture thinking, draw out the gifts in employees and others, leave memorable images and metaphors, introduce the power of stories, bring all the voices into the room and demonstrate through example that leadership is more than following a plan; it also involves sensing into the flow and energy of the moment and adjusting as we go.

As we talked together it became apparent that these conversations would embody many of the principles of craftwork I described earlier. In other words, craft is not limited to making things; it is integral to how we give shape, tone and structure to our learning environments as well.

Principles we considered included the following:

- We expected that, as facilitators, we were also learners and we would be transformed through these conversations.

- We focused the questions on seeing the big picture and taking the long view — on articulating the destiny and deeper purpose of the enterprise over the long term — rather than on short-term tactics or strategies.

- We wanted to encourage employees to reach for the impossible and not limit themselves to what they already knew how to do.

- We invited 150 employees from across multiple divisions as well as external stakeholders from other sectors globally to create opportunities for 'conceptual blending' — to discover how

separate ideas, points and cultural perspectives can coexist —
in order to imagine new possibilities and connections in the
spaces between.

- We recognized that to tap into these deeper aspirations, we
  would also need to connect with the inspiration of the founding story; these conversations would create a sense of place in
  the future by reconnecting with their sense of place in the past
  and the current environment.

- We focused on creating an environment that would invite a
  spirit of collaboration and bonding and create an open-end-
  ed schedule that would allow for ease of effort and minimum
  force.

- We created a warm, brightly lit, welcoming and natural environment with music that encouraged a lightness of being
  through relaxed, unfocused conversation. We knew the insights that would be of most value would come when we let go
  and stopped looking for them.

- While we had a detailed plan, we often adjusted it in practice based on following the lead of the moment for what was
  needed next.

- With the right environment, conversations can be more than
  simply exchanging information. They can be a powerful force
  for generating new insights when whole-mind thinking is encouraged. These conversations offered a pause — a stillpoint —
  in which to step back and look at the bigger picture, allowing
  leaders to locate their place in the larger context, invite a range
  of possibilities and establish new options for action.

In excerpts from his open letter of invitation to employees, Kumar
wrote,

Our greatest challenge is to define our future in a way that is aligned with our deepest goals and aspirations. We must ask, what is the destiny we see for our company that we would be most proud of? And how can our esteemed past inform our future? Our forefathers have created something that has endured the passage of time. How can we learn from these roots? And what is our gift? Imagine the power of an organization that not only understood the gift we individually brought but figured out how to unleash its power.

He concluded the invitation by saying, "Our journey begins today, not with meetings or schedules but with the dignity found in every conversation."

The Mythic
Landscapes of Place:

Four Archetypal Conversations

There was a time when the natural world was enchanted with exemplary figures who in their full presence served as wise guides to help make visible a hidden world of interconnection and wholeness. To build resilient neighbourhoods and communities we need to reacquaint ourselves with the essence of this mythic world again.

In our design thinking, we hoped to nourish an environment in which employees could imagine possibilities that went beyond an economic and tactical mindset, in which they became 'mythic-thinkers' who could see the broader, complex ecology of the organization, including its role in contributing to the health and well-being of the larger environment.

Scientist Erwin Lazlo writes that "there is a constant and intimate contact among things that co-exist and co-evolve in the universe — a sharing of bonds and messages that make reality a stupendous network of interaction and communication."

Through gathering together in this way, we hoped these leaders might, for even a moment, connect with this complex, elegant web of connections and communications through the conversations they would have together. To do so they would need to suspend their logical and analytic reasoning minds in order to bring to life their own capacities for mythic thinking.

To think mythically involves not only focusing on the immediate environment of cause and effect but shifting our focus to the larger system of patterns and flows in the human — and the more-than-human — community. Mythic thinking does this by gathering messages from diverse sources and bringing them into the best collective thinking they can achieve on any issue. This thinking takes into account that we have not one but multiple centres of influence. By taking these spheres of influence into our thinking we can provide leaders with informed insights regarding the complex matrix of networks and relationships. By grasping the whole system they can better understand the broader context in which they operate and at same time inspire strategies for how to change it.

While we could have introduced many questions, we chose to explore themes that held archetypal significance — that is, themes that are at the root of most wisdom traditions and a leader's instinctual life. These include the Destiny Story, the Design Story, the Aliveness Story, and the Heritage or Founding Story.

We also chose them because questions of aliveness, destiny, courage and legacy are the primary materials for so many of the stories we tell. They bring us home to ourselves. Many feel they are living outside their story now, uprooted, and led by rote in a flashlight world, their actions dictated by script, by credentials, by strategy or tactics, by our five-year plan or by what the expert says. Too often images that stories convey are too impractical to hold any real value and so are postponed for some later time.

We subscribe to the brilliance of this world by making absolute its qualities of purpose, direction, focus, willfulness, action and clear-sightedness. We miss how, when these qualities fall out of balance, they become absolutes, reinforced by the beliefs of perfection, absolute truth, separation, efficiency, scarcity and control. We hunger for what the wonder and sacredness of the candlelight brings — for a more soulful life that includes landscape, music, art, subtlety, nuance and the gifts of trust, silence, grace, surrender, connection and risk.

The light of the candle speaks to this more mythic life — one that addresses our own longing — and to the timeless needs and wisdom of the heart. The leader's work now is to engage the full ecology of human endeavour through finding the balance between the intellect's passion for strategy, action and outcome with the heart's affinity for enchantment and a disciplined unknowing.

To achieve this balance, the Greeks considered each place to be home to a god, and each place spoke to them out of the unique power, presence and character that that particular god possessed. As representatives of the eternal on earth, we were also gods. Walt Whitman said "we convince through our presence." As we embrace a more enchanted world, wherever we go, we *are* representatives of this eternal wisdom. It is the space between us that forms whenever we meet.

To participate in this exemplary world we cannot rely upon the intellect's understanding alone. Nor can we apply the same strategies to change our world that we used to create it. We will need to invite into our midst, and be guided by, these exemplars and respect them as the archetypal presences that shape the meta-narratives in our lives and, in so doing, re-enliven our own creative imagination.

So, in designing these events, implicit in our minds was a mythic map of the four archetypal patterns that hold the dynamic flow of conversation. Each of these exemplars serves as a significant marker on a leader's timeless journey toward discovering their natural place in the world.

THE SOVEREIGN

The Sovereign tells the story of destiny, hope and aspiration. In the Destiny Story we are made strong by drawing upon our own rootedness to place as the source of our prophetic voice. Our prophetic voice speaks out of a future made known to us long before it happens. Through acting in faith to our own call to adventure we discover the art of invisible intention and how this intention transforms scarcity into abundance and extends a spirit of blessing and goodwill to all within our realm. In this context the sovereign is the 'space holder' who invites and welcomes all the voices into the conversation and ensures they are heard.

THE WEAVER

The Weaver tells the story of magic, truth and possibility. The weaver knows we cannot control our future but we can design it. And designing our future is more powerful than trying to adapt or predict it. The weaver's story also reflects the truth of our current reality and is aligned with the leader's strength in seeing the tension in the relationship between the existing parts and the intricate patterning of the whole. It sees the expansion and potential of local wisdom and the constraints imposed upon it by current conditions. These leaders occupy the threshold of different realities and weave them together with ease, playfulness and a keen sense of grace. In order to overcome obstacles and find new ways forward, the weaver invites us to display our assumptions and certainties as well as our doubts and fears. The weaver also helps us in our journey by guiding us as we progress between the known and the unknown world.

THE ENCHANTER

The Enchanter tells the story of beauty, gifts, appreciation and inner seeing. As the source of our aliveness, the leader as the enchanter possesses the gift of seeing generously. They see the world through the lens of beauty, fulfillment, empathy and joy. This is the instinct for building connections and relationships that connect our place in the human dimension with nature, art and the larger-than-human world. The enchanter invites us into a space of deep listening so that we can hear not only what is said but also the other's request to be truly seen and understood — a request for listening with empathy that lies just behind the words. In our journey the enchanter also holds up the light of beauty that helps us find our way.

THE STEWARD

The Steward tells the story of our history, legacy and tradition. The Heritage Story casts the leader as the protector and integrator of the realm, drawing together and serving as the steward in conserving the wisdom of the past and the heritage accumulated over the ages. The protector's loyalty is to the seed that holds the code for the whole, honouring local traditions and nourishing our connection to a story that has been a source of teaching and wisdom for many years. It is done with a commitment to truth, courage, service and seeking the integrity of the whole. The steward is the protector who ensures each person is received with respect. The root of respect is to 'look again,' which means that each person receives a second opportunity to be known and understood. The steward also connects us with traditional sources of wisdom that will give us strength on our journey.

Consistent with our assumption that place matters, the first employee-engagement meeting included 150 participants invited from across multiple levels and positions in the company. The gathering was convened in the atrium of the Harold Washington Library in the heart of downtown Chicago. We crafted the space so that it would feel more like a market square or café filled with natural light, music, art-making, conversation and festivity.

To help a large, diverse group of leaders who are often overwhelmed by the pace of their work slow down and reflect more broadly on the big-picture "what if" questions, we needed to create a conducive atmosphere. And the atmosphere was to create a theatrical stage where they could all be players in re-imagining a work culture in which they could create together.

Then we could help them see their work from different perspectives. For example, questions of the future give them hope, enliven their aspirations and offer time to dream; questions of the past give them context and certainty; and questions of the present offer a sense of security and continuity. Leaders usually focus on one or two of these perspectives at any one time, or they think of them sequentially. But they will need to be in all three places at the same time if they are to navigate wisely in times of unpredictability and sudden change

THE DESTINY STORY: THE ART OF INVISIBLE INTENTION

It is out of our sense of belonging to a place that
we can more clearly see our destiny.

– Walter Brueggemann

The soul longs to reach out and make a home for its aspirations in the future through embracing its destiny. To shape our destiny is to do what is necessary, something that we were born to do, something that is not a matter of choosing but of bringing into being a course of action that has already been chosen for us. The Sovereign Archetype holds the key that opens this door into this future. In a world where everything is focused on short-term results and the bottom line, we may ask: What is our story and our place in the larger universe? Our destiny story is more than a vision composed of a list of possibilities. It is something heartfelt and purposeful we can breathe life into. In the machine age, this question might seem unimportant when compared to the practical quest for immediate goals and results.

As we enter a biological age, however, we are creating a dynamic field where the future will bring ideas, careers and possibilities for which we may not be prepared and have no language to describe. The limits of our language are also the limits of our world. A destiny conversation is both a process of connecting with our deeper purposes individually and collectively as well as an exercise in creating a new story and a language large enough to welcome a world yet to arrive.

Also, a conversation about our destiny story doesn't occur to create an ultimate goal or end state; instead, it serves as a powerful instrument to articulate our deepest vocation. The word vocation comes from *vocare*, which is the same root for "calling" and "voice." It is a conversation with the future that invites us to give voice to what it is we feel uniquely called to do. And because questions of destiny speak to a sacred call they take on the tone of the spiritual quest. In this context we might ask:

- What do we aspire to?

- What is the destiny story we most want to give voice to?

- What claims us?

- To what do we feel most beholden or connected to?

- What are we uniquely called to do, and what do we most aspire to be?

- What is the inner necessity that moves us forward?

Living into our destiny story is the work not of perfection but of possibility. The future cannot speak to us if our focus becomes the relentless search for perfection. The world of possibility is enlivened when we reach beyond what is implementable to what is imaginable. Lightly holding what we imagine allows breathing space for aligning our aspirations with the core purposes of our community or organization. By sketching out our desired future, we create a space for the future to speak to us. By inhabiting it *as if* it exists now, we are also making a place for our future in present time.

The word "we" is important. When a community connects with itself in creative ways, a new imaginative intelligence emerges. We need many eyes and ears on the future; it is far too large for any one person to discern alone. To create this image of our shared future, every voice is needed. When even one voice is silenced or sublimated, the world is missing a piece of the puzzle. We need all the voices for the full image of our shared destiny to be complete.

Our greater aspirations often fail because we don't have a language large enough to speak of them. By making a place to pause, to reflect, to ponder, to question, to imagine, to rethink and to restate what we aspire to, we are putting flesh on the words that collectively express the destiny we long to achieve. In making a home to receive and speak from the gift of our prophetic voice, we are creating the words as we speak. All transformation begins in language, so this work was engaging us in the higher mission of *language-making.*

Often the future we aspire to create cannot be achieved within the span of our own lifetime. Mythic stories unfold across the long arc of time. The future is also a story that must remain incomplete because it is not only for us to write, but also for others to share. We are making space in the future for others to occupy.

As such, destiny stories recognize and bless our deepest aspirations. They see and articulate the shared intention, aspirations and voice of the whole. This leads us to ask how we can encourage many eyes and ears to think large enough to create a home in the future that everyone can live into. While one person may serve as a memory-keeper of the past, no one person can hold the field for imagining the future. That is a quest we engage in together.

THE DESIGN STORY: BALANCING EXPANSION AND CONSTRAINT

If our destiny is the seed, then our current reality is the soil that holds within it the design for what wants to come next.

Once the call to fulfill our destiny is voiced, the journey begins. The Weaver Archetype holds the key to uncovering the truth in the moment. What factors in our reality might impede or enable our progress in realizing our destiny? We cannot realize our possible future without connecting to our current reality. So, in the design conversation, we ask,

- What is going on here?

- What enablers, difficulties, impediments, possibilities and challenges confront us?

- What seeds of potential or patterns in our current environment are aligned with our destiny?

- What needs to change, and what needs to be conserved?

- What is most difficult to talk about in our present situation?

- What are the natural limits in the system we need to consider?

- What more does the soil need for our aspirations to take seed and grow?

- How can we let go and let be?

- How can I let go and let be?

If our destiny is the seed, our current reality is the soil — it represents the 'local conditions' that balance our aspirations for *what if* with the immediate reality of *what is*. We can learn much from craftwork, which greatly values the presence of both expansion and constraint. Problems, obstacles and dilemmas act as stimulants that help transform the fire of inspiration so it burns with an even more intense light. The constraints of current reality, set in dynamic relationship to the forward motion of our aspirations, create a structural tension — a tension that will naturally seek resolution in the direction of what we seek to create. (Fritz, 1989.)

Tapping into the conditions of our local environment helps us search for latent patterns of opportunity, alternative courses of action, unlikely allies and hidden seeds of potential that can serve the pursuit of the destiny we want to create.

The design conversation therefore helps us see our present world from different angles and invites new possibilities in a spirit of generosity, detachment, perspective and novelty. It navigates the boundary between our known and unknown worlds, helping us see finely woven patterns of connection across different sectors that we might miss otherwise.

Conversations of constraint and potential also involve a careful reading of the complex web of relationships and the specifics of a place in order to see existing patterns that may enhance transformational shifts in the system as a whole.

Recognizing this, we become partners and allies with our destiny in ways that intellect, tactics and strategies alone cannot encompass. Our destiny is rooted in the regenerative power of the soil, intuitive wisdom, the powers of place, our heart's aspirations, and local knowledge. Living along the edges and tapping into the inherent aliveness of the moment is the foundation for forward movement behind any change that is to occur.

The Aliveness Story: The Art of Seeing Generously

Following the thread of our own aliveness is how we engage in a place-based world. In a time of dislocation, tapping into what leads us to feeling most alive instills a sense of hope and inspiration and leads us to where we most belong.

The Enchanter Archetype holds the key for tapping into our sense of aliveness in the moment. In the aliveness conversation, we ask,

- How can you be most yourself?

- What do you feel most connected to?

- When do you feel most at home?

- When do you feel most vital and alive and in the flow of things?

- What are your stories of a time when you can say *this* is what I was born to do?

This sense of aliveness has been a constant theme throughout *The Soul of Place*. This is because following the thread of our own aliveness is how we engage in a place-based world. Our aliveness is the core element connecting us to the way nature thinks; it is this innate attunement with the larger world that has contributed to our ability to survive and evolve.

So the aliveness conversation engages us in this timeless search for empathy and connection. It keeps us rooted in the quest to stay true to our own unfolding nature. And it hones our attention, which helps us discern the almost-imperceptible distinctions between things. The aliveness conversation also connects us to place, to nature, to inner stillness, to patience, and to a sense of the transcendent as this is experienced in the presence of strangers and new experiences.

In this sense, it fulfills what E. O. Wilson writes of as "biophilia" — the innate urge to connect with other forms of life (Wilson, 1984). In a time of dislocation, tapping into what makes us feel most alive and connected instils a sense of hope, belonging and inspiration. By acknowledging the centrality of *eros* — the sensual and the aesthetic aspect of our experience — the thread of aliveness brings us into a greater sense of balance and wholeness within ourselves and our world.

Most importantly, the thread of aliveness connects us to our innate gifts and signature strengths. So it is important to see the other's gifts generously in order to see our own greatness reflected back at us. When we see the greatness in the other, we can achieve more together. It is the inner strength of our gifts we draw upon that enables us to hold the creative tension between our destiny and our current reality. In other words, it is our gifts, which are our embodied strengths rather than our acquired skills — gifts given to us rather than skills acquired by us — that hold together the dynamic tension between the worlds of what-if and what-is. In this sense, leaders need to be multilingual as they hold the two competing realities of expansion and constraint together at the same time.

As Jaya Kumar said,

> In the context of the aliveness conversation, we can imagine the power of an organization that not only understands the gift we individually bring, it also recognizes and encourages its expression in a way that can release its full power. The bridge that holds the dynamic tension between our current reality and our destiny story are the gifts each one of us brings. This is the only way we can bridge the gap. And therefore, the

only way we can get to the destiny is to figure out the gifts our organization has and then ensure we create an environment that unleashes them.

By building this bridge between acknowledging our reality and reaching our destiny, the aliveness conversation highlights several aspects of craftsmanship. The first is educating the eye to see what truly holds a sense of energy and vitality. In a world of constant distraction, what is most present in the moment is easily missed.

The second is asking what we are willing to be open to. Can we unleash our curiosity and innate attraction even though it may lead us in unexpected directions, test our faith and raise our fear of the unknown? This ability to be open, to see things differently and to feel more aliveness and vitality in ourselves, can be disconcerting. It brings to the surface resistances we may have thought we had put to rest.

The third aspect of the aliveness conversation is being in the question, actively exploring what most intrigues us, opening new neural pathways, and staying ahead of 'the curve.' The purpose of each of these conversations is to stay connected to the edges of our own growing awareness so that we don't fall back into old habitual ways of thinking that are dictated by habit and routine.

The Heritage Story: Seeing the Roots that Hold the Whole

We need to celebrate our history while sketching a possible destiny that this history has presaged.

– George Will

The Stewardship Archetype holds the key to reconnecting with the roots from our past. In the heritage conversation, we may ask,

- Where is the place you come from?

- What is your legacy?

- What is the story you want to tell?

- How can you live in the integrity of your founding story?

- Who stands behind you, and in what ways are you truly unique?

Everyone comes from somewhere. Just as the acorn grows the oak tree, the place we come from holds the code for what we are destined to become.

This fourth story is the heritage conversation. It flows from the initial spark that was ignited from our connection to the natural world — the love, first aroused through an intimate encounter with the beauty of a place, that grows inward and outward over time. Our heritage story is the story of intimate connection with our original quest: to rediscover the place that satisfies this longing.

In our own founding story, we were wanderers in a world where every place felt like home. If only for a short time, every place we went we became. We became the flowers, the wind, the trees and the lakes and they in turn became part of us. We were not yet objects, categories or things but processes, experiences and flow. The world around us was also within us. We did not observe our world; we blended with and became what we saw. Over the ages, we accumulated and carried those ancient memories in stories and images that emerged out of the growth of our self-awareness; they became part of our collective DNA.

Even as we feel alone and disconnected, deep in our cellular memory we are integral with and belong to this great tidal surge of collective awareness that stretches across time.

Everything that originates in us, including our gifts, our aspirations and our latent potential and constraints, can be traced back to this essential connection we have with the earth as animate and alive, as home — a home that exists as a moral anchor and source of a deep life within us. This holds true both in our personal lives and in the founding or heritage stories that define the destiny of the organizations and communities we lead.

Through these conversations of who we are, we realize that a sense of place connects us not only to our desired future but also to the gifts from our past. This story has no ending; instead, it teaches us how to create new beginnings and how to join the stream of the larger story, demonstrating how we can unlock the promise within us by connecting to the rich heritage and wisdom of our storied past. In this way, we can draw the best from our traditions and carry them forward with us.

Our earliest memories, often formed while we were in our mother's arms, recapture in the sensory imagination some of the intimate encounters with the 'inscape' of our world. Soil, touch, warmth, moisture, wind, light and water, including tastes and smells, are constant reminders of how and where we experienced our first encounters with place. It is this deep affection for place that nurtures our love affair with the world.

We each have these places, perhaps long forgotten, that live in us still — places that press upon our consciousness, places that seek to be remembered and live through us again. Places we cannot return to but may grow out from. Places that give rise to experiences that cannot be adequately described in words.

These encounters with place are not a call to busyness or action but instead to a quieting of the mind and the resting of the soul so we may see the world in a fresh light. Reconnecting with our roots as well as our future is the first work of placemaking.

While these four directions gave shape and structure to our conversations, *how* we talk together was equally important. The roots of this practice also have ancient beginnings.

OUR OLDEST STORY OF PLACE:

DIALOGUE AND THE HERITAGE OF THE CIRCLE

*There are only two or three human stories, and they go on
repeating themselves as fiercely as if they had never
happened before. Like the larks in this country, that have
been singing the same five notes over thousands of years.*

– Willa Cather

One of those timeless stories that has been singing the same notes
for thousands of years is our life in the circle. The art of listening
and speaking is one of our oldest stories of coming together. The
central structure for this form of meeting, which came to be known
as dialogue, is the circle.

Lakota Elder Black Elk once said, "Everything the power of the
world does is done in a circle." And the most natural form of expressing the power of the circle is dialogue. This form of 'circular living'
has been at the root of engaging the work of the human imagination since the beginning of time. The circle has power because once
formed, no matter how strong the voices, its structure remains
unbroken. The circle cannot be divided. It is a symbol of wholeness
that has sustained us and our stories across the arc of time. And no

one, no matter how intelligent they are, is more intelligent than the collective intelligence of the circle. This may be explained by the notion that no one in the circle is higher or lower than another. Everyone is equal and every voice matters. Like the sweetgrass stalk, when we are alone we are fragile and break easily but when we are in the circle together we are unbreakable. The centre of the circle is like the skin of the drum. When it is pulled taut, it serves as our third ear, amplifying our ability to hear messages from the future that we cannot hear when we are alone.

In dialogue there is often more listening than talking. Through deep listening together we create a circle of vulnerability and trust where everyone belongs. The wider the circle, the more resilient this place of trust can become. And for the circle to be resilient, we need to be open with one another. We need to accept new possibilities and let go of our habitual instinct to control the process. By doing so, we will receive something from the circle itself that may shift how we see ourselves and how we view our world.

The root of "dialogue" comes from the Greek *dia* and *logos*, which means *meaning moving through*. Dialogue helps us break off from the conflicted life of separation and individualism and create a transformative space for the voice of the imagination to be heard once again.

While I have convened the circle as a place for transformative learning for many years, my first experiences in creating a cultural transformation of place through shifting the patterns of communication from debate to dialogue occurred in an endeavour with Shell Oil when I was part of a small multi-disciplinary team with the Dialogue Project at the MIT Center for Organizational Learning. The project was framed as an experiment. The goal was to create a place in which a new set of values and communications would engender new respect among leaders and within the larger work environment and among their community of stakeholders and partners as well.

As part of our work, I had the opportunity to hear a talk by Philip J. Carroll, president and CEO of Shell Oil, as he thought about his learning journey. He included his personal experiences and challenges in undertaking a corporate-wide renewal strategy to transform Shell into a learning and development organization that fostered greater sharing and collaboration.

Shell at that time, through its investment in transformational learning processes, sought to move from being one of the weakest to one of the strongest of the seven sisters that made up the competing resource companies. Carroll's reflections on what it would take to create an informal culture where employees could experience the value of shifting their perspective from driving results to also building relationships through dialogue shone a new light on how to create a story of place and placemaking within a high-pressure corporate environment.

For us it was also an experiment in exploring placemaking in the presence of two competing worldviews. How would the introduction of a circular culture based on building relationships and promoting greater intuition, creativity and fluidity impact a linear culture that measured progress solely in economic and financial terms? Our partners within the company were asking themselves similar questions.

In reflecting on the culture, Carroll spoke about how, as engineers and scientists, they took professional pride in advocating and debating the merits of their own ideas and pointing out the deficiencies of their opponent's point of view. They were at home with their certainties and accustomed to functioning in a world that was absolute and finite. They rarely listened, asked questions or appreciated how others perceived and thought about the issues at hand. He admitted that this pattern of adversarial communication at the top of the organization set the tone of the culture throughout the system. In short, they were accustomed to seeing their world in discreet, distinct and tangible forms. It was a world of things rather than relationships.

His observations are not unique to one team or one company — they describe the prevailing mindset of most institutions as well as the dominant worldview of the western world. His observations help explain how this institutional mindset can easily disable our efforts to introduce more circular relationship-based cultures in most work environments. It is the central story of our time, the roots of which can be traced back to the conflicts between aboriginal civilizations based on the Sacred Circle of life and their devastation as a result of the arrival of more linear-based societies from Europe hundreds of years ago.

The paradox is that, to create circular communities that value relationships and respect, we will need to learn to think like aboriginals again.

It is interesting that in the western mind *distinct* itself implies division. The work of these engineers and scientists involved reducing and dividing their world into parts, including separate compartments, silos, objects and processes. When we see with the detachment of a highly focused attention without also seeing the depth and context of the big picture behind it, it is natural that we debate what we see. With such narrow vision, we will each naturally see different things.

To see the world dialogically involves learning from what is forming rather than from what is already formed. We learn to soften our vision and become more literate in a subtle language that is more suggestive and implicit.

Then we can learn to focus our attention on not knowing — a state of mind that encourages us to not only *look at* but to *see through* an idea in order to appreciate the qualities and possibilities that lie beyond. We strive to engage an idea based not only on its face value but also on the framework and depth of what lies behind and around it.

In this context, dialogue involves inhabiting rather than simply observing a space. When we inhabit a space our primary concern is to care for it in some way — to ensure that it feels natural, hospitable and welcoming, that it fulfills the needs of not only the mind but also the heart and the body. Places rarely feel natural when we are trying to organize, structure or control them in a deliberate way or when they only serve a utilitarian purpose that does not engage both the feeling and thinking aspects of our nature.

If there were to be significant changes in the science-bound culture of Shell, people would need to begin by engaging with one another in a significantly different way. This transformation started with the creation of a co-governance structure in which each vice-president was responsible for their functional area and also served as a member of a stewardship group, set up as a governing council to serve the whole enterprise.

"I needed my vice-presidents to be stewards along with myself to look out for the well-being and health of the whole of the enterprise, not just their part of it," Carroll said. To transform the business, they needed to not only compete with one another for resources for their departments but also see the big picture and look out for and have respect for each other.

This restructuring of the business made it possible for Shell executives to shift their focus from debate to dialogue as they deliberately learned to listen and understand each person's unique point of view. This wasn't easy; it turned their familiar world upside down. Turning to dialogue from a world of abstractions and absolutes, they could never quite know something completely because it was always evolving and thus always incomplete.

In dialogue, comprehension is formed not through abstractions but through experience. To comprehend something, we need to feel it first. We often try to explain a world that we would do better to simply savour and wonder at. Wonder reminds us there is a part of the world that has not yet been fully accounted for. It connects us to the sense of mystery, awe, possibility and constructive perplexity. This perplexity may actually embody more insight than all the solutions we have at hand. The learning journey is more important than the arrival as we try to understand a world that can never be fully understood.

In contrast, the mark of objectivity, abstraction or detachment is to not be moved by anything. This is the goal of debate — to be a detached and immoveable object so we can maintain our sense of detached bemusement. We attempt to diminish and demystify in order to reduce the full presence of the other. When they are diminished, they serve not as an equal partner but as an object of our influence and persuasion.

In dialogue the essence of the other is crucial. Their full presence allows our subjective experience and ability to flow and blend with them. The less they are, the less we may become. Ultimately, making meaning visible involves not yielding to but engaging with others so that together we may come to see what we cannot see on our own.

In other words, truth does not reveal itself through our willful grasping for it, or from our detachment and objectivity, but from waiting upon and engaging with it. We might think of truth as a shy animal that hides away in the bushes. If we search for it too forcefully, it retreats deeper into the forest and cannot be found. Instead, we need to coax it out into the open. In this quest, uncertainty replaces certainty. As we improve our skills in engaging with a force that cannot be pinned down or contained, the fixed and static turns out to be a constantly changing, fluid phenomenon.

In debate we try to bend others to our will; in dialogue we blend with others in order to see a greater whole. In this spirit, dialogue is rooted in the work of craft and connects us to this same second nervous system. Our attention is directed to the space between. In dialogue practice, this in-between space is located in the impersonal centre of the circle, where insights may come from any one person, rather than at the front of the room.

We often overlook the luminous power of this second nervous system to transform group learning and create fields for innovation. All life is movement, yet when we speak we don't think of group processes as a metaphor for movement. Our primary metaphors for movement come from the physical body; they are muscular and skeletal. We understand the body primarily through images of rigidity and resistance and the interaction between sinews, nerves, bones, density and structure.

But the much larger part of the body is made up of water molecules and connective tissue. This second nervous system is cellular rather than muscular and it moves in space through a blending of fluid motion rather than the force of effort. In other words, the ancient DNA, in which we were not separate and discreet but intimately attuned to our world, is still very much a part of the make-up of our nervous systems today. The practice of dialogue leads us toward becoming re-initiated to this more subtle body.

Understanding this alternate aspect of body structure is helpful in thinking about the distinctions between dialogue and debate. The muscular body, which is more individually oriented and transactional, moves in space with greater force of effort than the cellular or fluid body of the dialogue circle.

Processes such as listening, reflection and speaking out of the moment shift the density of a group from this rigid, individually focused muscular structure to something more spacious and flexible.

We notice this change most clearly in our tone of voice. When we are in the cellular body, the sound of our voices shifts from our throat and chest to a space deeper in the solar plexus. As it does so, our voices soften and slow down; our words form more slowly as our thoughts and feelings become more attuned to what is occurring in the moment.

This metaphor of the body, in contrast to the workings of the abstract mind, may be at the core of the distinction between debate and dialogue. Where dialogue is fluid and relational, playing in the in-between spaces, debate focuses on what has utility and what is most useful. It is self-referential, so its primary focus is not the other person but oneself.

Debate is also more muscular in emphasizing the rightness of one's position. Debate tends to reduce our sense of reality as we become more narrowly focused on the repetition of our own concepts and abstractions. Dialogue, on the other hand, seeks to expand our horizons and sense for what is real according to the place we occupy in the world. Our relationship to this place will in turn shape our experiences and aspirations.

Carroll admitted this was a steep learning curve. He and his leaders struggled to learn a new way of communication. "We felt like we were five years old again," he said. "It was very humbling but absolutely necessary if we were to seriously address the fragmentation and divisiveness that was undermining the effectiveness of the enterprise."

As Shell Oil president and CEO, he knew that to become a truly developing and evolving organization they would need to see themselves not only as strong, independent and individually directed contributors but also as collaborators and networkers who could build relationships and access a collective intelligence. This would help them achieve together what they could not accomplish on their own.

As proof of their success, Shell went on to develop collaborative partnerships with competitors and communities in order to create an ecosystem that could address complex challenges and capitalize upon their partners' diverse strengths. The dialogue process and learning in the circle helped them adapt to managing greater complexity; they sought balance by encouraging diversification while ensuring that each was integrated and connected to the overall core vision.

D. H. Lawrence in his poem "The Third Thing" wrote, "Water is H2O; hydrogen two parts, oxygen one. But there is a third thing that makes it water, and nobody knows what *that* is."

"This way of talking together, it transformed our business," Carroll said in his reflections. "That said, as an engineer, we still don't know what *it* is!"

Third Places:

Nourishing the Roots of Resilient Communities

*The atom locks up two energies but it is the third
thing present which makes it an atom.*

– D. H. Lawrence

We still don't know what "*it*" is. But to find it we need to look to the overlap, the space between two poles, where two or more worlds rub together and create a magic that transforms the other two.

When we connect with this inexplicable third thing, we are touched by another in ways that open us to the magic of the unexpected. This openness also unleashes a subtle power through which we discover what contributes to building innovation and resilience in our organizations and communities over the longer term.

Phil Carroll and his executive team transcended the tensions between maintaining the status quo on the one hand and expanding upon their own individual self-interest on the other. In so doing they opened a third possibility, which was to act collectively for the greater good of the enterprise.

The third thing is the domain of luminosity. It is often found in some aspect of place that has been neglected or overlooked. The power of the centre in dialogue practice has often been overlooked in favour of teaching and presenting from the front of the room. In our communities, the third thing is found in 'third places,' which include those aspects of the built environment that have been neglected or overlooked but bristle with potential energy — places like alleyways between old buildings, vacant lots, and hallways.

Recently I facilitated a conversation with the board of a medical healing centre in a community nearby. The centre is unique in that its governing board includes First Nations, francophone and anglophone members, who make up the three founding cultures in the community.

I made the rounds with the executive director looking at potential spaces in which to meet. There was the main meeting room with projectors and screens and large, heavy tables. And we looked at the lunch room, where we might fit in several small tables. Then we looked at the hallway and I said, "Let's meet here."

The focus of our meeting was to invite each person to share their personal and community story of place — a conversation across generations and cultures that they had not yet had. The hallway was a neglected space — people passed through but did not dwell there — so it offered a space for a different and unique conversation that was neither business nor social in focus. It offered something that belonged in the in-between space.

Following the meeting, the director wrote to say that they affected themselves and others in the story-sharing in ways he had not seen before. Reaching this depth may have been partly due to embracing the 'it' — that is, to meet in a neutral space, much like the centre of a dialogue circle, that had not yet been claimed for other purposes.

Henry David Thoreau once said, "I have three chairs in my house, one for solitude, two for friendship and three for society."

Those places where we find the third chair hold the greatest potential for transformation.

Going a little further afield, Steve Jobs was a student of third places and placemaking. He believed that the right kind of building can do great things for nourishing a culture. Simplicity of design flowed into the informal and functional simplicity of his living environment. The buildings he worked in, particularly in the early years, looked meagre and stunted and were often located in remote areas, separate and apart from the busy mainstream of corporate operations. But it was here where he could, with the collaboration of a small creative team, build soil that would support radically new product innovations.

Pixar constructed a huge building around a central atrium. The topsoil here was found in this central and informal meeting place, which served as the commons. It was designed to encourage random encounters and spontaneous conversation. If an environment doesn't encourage this, Jobs believed, you will lose innovation and magic that is sparked by such serendipity.

Jobs said, "I want to create a 'place between' where engineers are working in tandem with designers." (Isaacson, 2011.)

Walter Isaacson, in his biography of Jobs, writes about how his heroes were people who could stand at the intersection of aesthetics and technology. It was building these bridges across sectors, disciplines and worldviews — spaces pregnant with possibility — that Jobs was most passionate about. If we extend the metaphor of topsoil further, we can imagine that it exists as a life-force constellation bursting with energy, sitting at the intersection where any two or more forces come together for any reason — in the natural order of things it is where earth and heaven meet.

Isaacson discovered while writing his biographies of Jobs, Benjamin Franklin and Albert Einstein that the creative force they held in common occurred at the interface where the humanities and sciences met. When these forces came together in one strong personality, or cohesive group, it was key to creating innovative economies (Ibid, 2011). This explains why leaders who have excelled in more than one discipline tap into this constellation of energy that helps them see possibilities others may miss.

To build resilient environments, leaders will benefit from creating third places in which to meet — physical places outside the normal daily routine of work, family and friends. (Oldenburg, 2000.) These are spaces where unfamiliar forces rub up against each other. They take us out of the familiar because they are unscripted and free of routine associations. These places also open us to the kind of newness, curiosity and deep and playful exploration upon which creating a regenerative culture depends. They are places where we can build topsoil as we find new ways of meeting and talking together.

The New Yorker magazine recently reported on a study done by sociologist Eric Klinenberg that describes how the resilience needed to cope with natural and man-made disasters will be based not only on physical infrastructure but also on relationships. To build resilient relationships, we will need to give closer attention to the importance of 'social infrastructure' — people, places and informal social networks — through which we can build the social capital, cohesion and support to cope with major stressors on the community in the future.

When he examined the experiences of two adjacent neighbourhoods following the Chicago heatwave of 1995, Klinenberg found that the difference between Englewood, which recorded a fatality rate of 33 per 100,000 residents, and Auburn Gresham, with a rate of 3 per 100,000 residents, was dramatic.

He explained the difference by noting that Auburn Gresham had very healthy and vibrant third spaces. They had sidewalks, so people could walk to stores and restaurants, connect with community organizations, block clubs, church groups — in these social networks and associations, people looked out for each other. They knew their neighbours. Living in Auburn Gresham was the "rough equivalent of having a working air-conditioner in each room," Klinenberg wrote. (*The New Yorker*, January 2013.)

In adjoining Englewood, there was no good soil; people had abandoned the neighbourhood. They were vulnerable not only because they were poor but because the community over 30 years had lost 50 percent of its residents and, with this, most of its commercial outlets as well as its social networks. It had lost the richness of its collective memory and history.

Building these complex social networks through nurturing third places in communities is the equivalent to building healthy topsoil on the land. They remind us of the fragility of place — that the life force that creates and sustains the land, or the social fabric of a community, is often only six inches deep, yet the health of this six inches is crucial. It is all that separates us from the sudden collapse of physical and social ecosystems and their opposite, which is realizing their potential to prosper and grow.

Barry Lopez writes, "Topsoil is always enriched by all the things that die and enter into it. It keeps the past not as history or memory but as a richness and new possibility — its fertility is always building up out of death to promise." (Lopez, 2001.)

Our attention to place and placemaking, then, is not optional. A place-based perspective makes the difference between those who have deep roots in their communities and those who don't. How we find and develop these roots is part of what it means to create the resilience of a place-based economy.

In our Banff forum on the power of place, Nick Nissley, at that time the executive director of Banff Leadership Development, shared what another parent at his daughter's soccer game said to him: "We should have our town meetings here at the soccer field. There are 150 parents and 100 kids in this field, and we're lucky if we have five people show up for a town meeting. But here, half the town is standing around the soccer field. And in 45 minutes, people are exchanging intimate conversations with numerous people they may not always meet up with during the day." (Banff Forum, 2010.)

Colleague Judy Brown, a poet and leadership educator, said in response, "I have been thinking a lot about the way in which strangers often bring us important news of the world and sometimes actually call out something they see in us that otherwise goes unseen. I have been thinking about the way in which the creation of space is often a meeting space of strangers. Images like oases, intersections, and journeys where we cross paths with each other."

Reclaiming the Commons:

Healing the Hollowed-out Centre of Our World

This is an age of vast promise, an age of collaboration – an age of sharing and understanding the new power of the commons.

– Don Tapscott

We live in a world out of balance. To find a new centre, we need to balance consumption with conservation — to acknowledge that, when we take from the whole, we also must give back to the whole. While the notion that setting half aside for nature has been explored in relation to the preservation of natural and wild places (Brown, 2013), it also applies to how we seek to preserve the third spaces between our public and private lives in the social sphere.

These oases, intersections and journeys where we cross paths between the public and private places have historically been known as the commons. We could add to this list of commons places the front porch, the village green, the plaza, the library, the art gallery, the public square, the cafeteria, the waiting room, the local mall, the chapel, the park bench, as well as time spent in nature, listening to music, admiring beauty and the presence of natural light.

Many find themselves in a busy, placeless, hollowed-out world — a world where, in the words of poet William Butler Yeats, "The ceremony of innocence is drowned; / The best lack all conviction, / while the worst / Are full of passionate intensity."

In a world where we have hollowed out the centre of our lives and communities, we hunger for places of meaning where we can live a life of significance and create new spaces and places where we can gather. These new centres include welcoming opportunities for chance encounters with "strangers" who meet at the intersections across perceived differences and boundaries. Within these places we enter a pause, a time-out, a moment of suspension to be with others and ourselves in a different, more spontaneous and unique way. More broadly, we might say these places are any space in which we feel calmer, clearer and happier, brighter, whether it is being absorbed in a book on the floor of a bookstore, sitting by a waterfall, being immersed in a conversation or a piece of music — experiences writer and monk David Steindl-Rast describes as "the kind of happiness that doesn't depend on what happens."

This is the subtle power of third places. They provide the opportunity to see the familiar through fresh eyes. Because they are not fully planned, organized, or strategic in orientation, they offer neutral, safe and creative places for regenerative change to occur. They provide unique opportunities to be spontaneous and energized by the presence of the creative, the unknown and the unexpected.

Most importantly, these third places offer an opening to a unique social institution known as the commons. The commons is the bridge between public and private space. The commons offers a space for the thread of fellowship and collective consciousness in which the rich diversity of voices that has been with us through the fullness of time can be in dialogue together again.

The root of the word *commons* comes from *ko*, which means "together," with the Greek *moin* meaning "held in common." Interestingly, it also has a corresponding root in *mei*, which means to move, as in "meaning moving through," and also in *munus*, which means a "service performed for the community or municipality." (Snyder, 1990.)

The commons is the in-between place in our community, a place of *at homeness* that exists outside our normal daily routine of work, family and friends, such as the soccer field in the earlier example. These places are unscripted and free of routine associations. As Jonathon Row in his essay "The Hidden Commons" writes, "A commons has a quality of just being there. Generally there are no formal rules to regulate the internal workings of the commons." (Rowe, 2001.) The commons is also a space of disinterest. That is, because it is not owned or claimed by anyone, it is uniquely free to be fully itself. Rowe highlights another characteristic of the commons: it is full of serendipity. Rowe writes, "The commons engages people as wholes, and this tends to produce a multiplier of benign effects, especially in terms of social cohesion and trust." (Ibid.)

In this context, the commons offers a powerful unifying narrative for how we may weave our fragmented world back together again. Anything that belongs to all of us belongs in the commons. It represents the vast realm of our shared heritage, including the atmosphere, the waters, the air we breath, languages, cultures, human wisdom, neighbourhoods and the solace of public gathering places. For all of time, the commons has been the forum where the most essential, and least tangible, aspects of our nature, including our subjective experience, our authentic presence, our way of speaking truly and our uniqueness, is held as being imperishable. In short the commons, because it is the place where everyone belongs, is where we are protected from the wasting disease of our own loneliness and invisibility.

And, yet, while the commons is always with us, we rarely see it. As a consequence we have, for many years, drawn from our common pool resources and hidden wealth without restraint.

Perhaps because we have forgotten how to see the commons for what it truly is, we may consider our time in the commons as a diversion or escape from the necessities of our day-to-day world. To reclaim the commons is to acknowledge our responsibility to it and to its essential role in fostering resilient communities and re-imagining our personal and collective future during times of chaotic events or sudden change. As such, the commons opens us to a kind of newness, curiosity and deep and playful exploration upon which building social capital and cohesion begins.

In the context of nurturing the quality of place, we may ask about the health of our commons. That is, what is the health of our relationships, including the trust and goodwill and shared resources we have created together? And where is the blank canvas, the open space that is not owned or controlled by others, on which we can co-create possibilities?

Wherever we go, we *are* the commons. It is the space between that forms whenever we meet in a spirit of conviviality and dissolves when we are apart. It is the space of reciprocity in which we existed and thrived for thousands of years as we confronted the daily mystery of the universe. The commons as a space for building meaningful relationships and seeing the gifts in the other is also a space for life. According to David Bolier in his new book, *Think Like a Commoner*, this relates to another possible root of the commons, which is *munus*, meaning both "gift" and "counter gift." Bolier writes, "We need to recover a world in which we all receive *gifts* and all have *duties*." In this way the commons not only serves as a way of managing resources wisely, it is also the path to deepen our own 'common' humanity collectively.

This intimate correspondence with our social and more-than-human world filled us with a profound joy. It was what made us fully human. It was the unfathomable wonder of being present to the mystery of an invisible world that existed side by side with the difficulties and demands of our day-to-day reality. Restoring the commons space may be the true work of *Homo faber* as the maker, the craftsperson, artist and placemaker — and the architect of collaboration — who crafts the commons spaces again.

One of the difficulties of the commons is that, like topsoil, it also hides in plain sight. While the commons is always with us, we are not always aware of it. The busyness of our world often blinds us to the deeply subjective experiences that bubble up in the spaces between the notes. The success of early cultures was that these spaces *were* their world. What could not be seen or understood was not considered a threat or adversary, but a gift. And because it was a gift, to be in the commons always involved the ritual act of giving back.

When we shift our emphasis from a solely economic perspective to one that is more ecological and place-based, the commons can then tap into and re-energize the process of building connections, acknowledging our gifts, recognizing the power and significance of place, finding our voice and discovering renewed strength and confidence in our vulnerability and not knowing.

The future invests always in the imagination. Unlike the intellect, the imagination never grows old in its quest for beauty and aliveness. Our destiny depends on recognizing this vast, untapped power. And one of the ways we amplify the creative power of the commons is through the mythic life of Carnival and transformative celebration.

The spirit of Carnival connects us with how nature itself creates and sustains life. By reconnecting with the mythic roots of our own poetic life, we become allies with each other and our destiny in ways that the intellect, tactics and strategies alone cannot encompass.

Carnival awakens our intuitive wisdom, the powers of place, our heart's desires, our greatest aspirations, the gifts each person brings and the collective intelligence that has called us to be together on this journey again.

FINALLY SHALL COME THE POET:

SINGING THE NEW WORLD INTO EXISTENCE

After the noble inventors, after the scientist,
the chemist, the geologist, ethnologist,
Finally shall come the Poet worthy that name;
The true son of God shall come singing his songs.

– Walt Whitman

One of the ways we reclaim and heal the hollowed-out centre of our world is to celebrate it. In Toronto there is a place named Mabelle Park that for years had been an empty scrap of land between two community-housing apartment buildings in the northwest section of the city. It is an example of one of the neglected third spaces we explored earlier. It served mostly as a short-cut to a subway stop and was a popular destination for muggers.

"There was a wading pool, and some elegant trees. But no one sat beneath them. The shade was the domain of unfriendly people, likely to mug or thump you." (Porter, *Toronto Star*, 2013.) Then a group of artists arrived in the area and started offering art classes.

They started "to slowly curate changes to the space. They added a brick oven for pizzas and a fire pit for cooking Iftar feasts — the evening break-fast meals during Ramadan… They also installed some garden plots and three wooden benches engraved with sentences such as 'she was the one' (each of the three benches had a place name) taken from conversations with locals." (Ibid.)

This may be what separates a good park from a great park, Porter noted. Good parks are where people come to walk dogs and sit on benches. Great parks go one step further. They are the home for Carnival. That is, as Porter writes, they are "places you can also meet people in… listening to live music or pushing your kid on a swing. Great parks are community slow cookers" — places for the sharing of stories and making memories together.

This is how a place is transformed. It is signalled through the return of the poet. The poet offers words of hope and a language of welcome, not words of despair. The poet represents the mythic, archetypal energies of joy, imagination and creativity. An invitation is issued to throw off the constraints and fears of the past and celebrate our life anew.

Whether we think of this occasion as Carnival or Festival or Ritual or Ceremony of some form, it is an energy that signals the reversal of formal authority and the upturning of our daily life. This is the call of our time. If in other great times past we called upon the accomplishments of inventors, economists, scientists and technologists, it is unique to our time that we call upon the mythic world of the artist, the craftsperson, the poet and prophet to bring forth those green shoots, bursting with energy of possibility, upon which the more intuitive and imaginative "I am"-ness of our world can be celebrated again.

In our busy time-bound and analytical world — a world in which we have no time for the inner life — art reconnects us to the mythic experience of faith, beauty, mystery, stillness and the joyful experience of time out of time itself. Most importantly, it invites us to suspend our attachments in order to create a learning field that is spacious, celebratory, integrative and whole.

It is this that leads the way to the surge of ecstatic expression in the celebration of public life we know as Carnival.

The roots of Carnival come out of West Africa. The word itself means "a farewell to flesh." It is a time of merry-making but also a time to throw off the old flesh in order to grow a new skin and make life anew.

Through the disruption to our daily routine, Carnival offers an anti-dote to a life out of balance. While these surges of ecstatic joy may feel threatening and uncontrollable — and in their extreme may lead us down a path of excess — without Carnival the world would be a poorer place. We would have lost our capacity for large-scale disruptive, joyful and transformational change.

CARNIVAL AND THE ART OF TRANSFORMATIVE CELEBRATION

If there is a future wave of wellness on this planet, of harmony, of peace, of an end to war, of mutual understanding, of equality, of fairness... I expect it will come from the artists.

– Karl Paulnack, 2004

This is a time of an expansion of consciousness. We are at the early edge of one of these big transformative shifts when the cultural landscapes of place are undergoing major changes. We experience it as a mounting pressure that may lead to the breakdown of existing structures and the unleashing of a global flow of new ideas, innovations and collaborative possibilities. These radical shifts may serve to bring out the deep skills of craft and the regenerative power of place within each of us as we learn through our own art how to participate in this emerging new world order. The spirit of Carnival reconnects us with these deep roots of place, which in turn inspires celebration.

Carnival lifts us up in a wave; its underlying philosophy is one of contagious and spontaneous joy. As the source of regeneration, Carnival represents the shift from the principles of stability and closure to one of constant flux and possibility. It is a fluid rather than fixed way of allowing our felt life to flow through.

Carnival often comes during times of great disruption, when there is a surge of energy so strong we may fear being swept away. Carnival can be best understood as the counterpoint to the world of official and dominant hierarchical order. It is a very particular form of energetic expression of the imagination that has been mostly silenced in hierarchical life. A world of duty, order and strategy does not give permission or a place for joy, for longing and for the feeling life.

In place of the sensuality and the celebration of abundance, hierarchy promotes the principle of efficiency at any cost, of scarcity, and the fear that enough is never enough. In this respect, hierarchy is a model of consumption, not of regeneration. A rule-bound world dismisses hope and aspiration as illusion and suspends imagination and the felt life of community.

In this context, Carnival can be seen as subversive. It awakens a neglected element in consciousness — an element that, when brought to awareness, will take us to a higher level of integration and wholeness. While embracing this new consciousness is vital to the evolution of consciousness, it cannot be prescribed. The way forward often enters our awareness only when we are willing to acknowledge our own vulnerability and embrace the elements that are most in shadow or unknown to us.

This may account for our fear of Carnival. It is a disruptive force that can turn our life upside down and, in so doing, transform the place we are in. At the present time, the most neglected element in our culture is our mythic life. We resist the unknown, the mystery, the ambiguity, the loss of control and certainty that are often associated with the adjustments to living a mythic life. And the mythic life — this sense that there is a hidden wholeness behind all things — is encountered most frequently in the arts.

Oliver Sachs writes in his book *Musicophilia,*

The primal role of music is to some extent lost today, when we have a special class of composers and performers, with the rest of us often reduced to passive listening. We have to go to a concert, or a church, or a musical festival to… recapture the collective excitement and bonding of music. In such a situation… there seems to be an actual binding or 'marriage' of the nervous systems. (Sachs, 2008.)

The binding together of our nervous systems, the experience of collective excitement — even rapture, and letting oneself go — this is the language of hospitality that Carnival calls us to. It is a return to that time when music and the arts played a much more imaginative and integral role in public life, not only as celebration for musical plays and religious festivals but also in daily ritual. Above all, it was a shared performance, not something we listened to passively.

The arts were the glue that brought us together and through which we experienced our common humanity even in the midst of hardship and uncertainty. To go forward we need to re-engage with mystery and ambiguity, with slowing down, with finding our own music and authentic voice. It is a shift in which we are witnessing the disruption of old structures and giving birth to the new.

But to give birth to the new may also stir our insecurities, for, among other things, Carnival is the travelling circus. It passes through town and then disappears in the night. Keeping our appointment with Carnival may change our life.

This is the power of Carnival. While we often associate it with displays of drunkenness and excess, we need to redefine Carnival more broadly as representing the force of art and nature that rises up from the ground deep beneath our feet, throws off the old order and brings forth new levels of wholeness and integration. It can be a positive transformative energy that remakes and transforms any place we are in.

Carnival is also a metaphor for the embodiment of experience. Its origins are found in empathic communications deeply connected to the body. The two core practices that help us access the life of the body are music and language. When I ask groups to reflect and share stories about their relationship to place, to beauty, to courage and gifts and to a sense of calling or vocation they struggle, often the questions are too abstract and ambiguous and they find themselves at a loss for words.

"Close your eyes and listen for a moment," I suggest. Then I play music and within moments the words flow like a torrent. Images and metaphors come to their blank page like a flood. It is a reminder that the emotional origins of an imaginative language begin in music. When language is separated from music and art, it shifts from the domain of rhythm, sensing and feeling to the visual domain. Our orientation also shifts to something more abstract: a form of communication limited to single meanings and one modality.

This emphasis on the bodily origin of music and language, which the spirit of Carnival returns to us, has been lost in our analytic age. The trend since the advent of the industrial age has been to repudiate our embodied being in favour of a more abstracted mechanistic-like version of ourselves, which has taken hold in popular thinking.

Carnival represents the disruption of this formal and abstracted life in favour of a multiplicity of voices and meanings. When we convene large group gatherings and introduce art in the form of movement, music, story, painting and song, we reintroduce the transformative symbols of the mythic world. We invite others to come on a journey with us, to enter into a place of enchantment, and with this the suspension of belief. The presence of streaming colours, bountiful banquets and luminous living spaces invites the throwing off of the old and the taking up of the new with the contagious joy it brings.

Carnival is an invitation to relocate the centre of our attention from ourselves and our self-interest to an interest in a place larger than ourselves — an essential struggle in which, in the process, some more limiting aspects of ourselves may die in order for a larger definition of our place in the world to emerge.

This process of giving new authority to the feeling life is the goal of Carnival. It re-engages and reunites art and nature with community and with life. Art reconnects us to another source of life that is not bound in the official world but in our common citizenship and humanity. This has always been the ancient wisdom Carnival celebrates and to which we may once again subscribe. (8)

As composer and writer Karl Paulnack says,

> If there is a future wave of wellness on this planet, of harmony, of peace, of an end to war, of mutual understanding, of equality, of fairness, I don't expect it will come from a government, a military force or a corporation. I no longer even expect it to come from the religions of the world… if there is to be an understanding of how these invisible, internal things should fit together, I expect it will come from the artists. (Paulnack, 2004.)

DEEP SONG:

DISCOVERING THE SOURCE OF ALIVENESS
WITHIN OURSELVES

whatever you have to say, leave
the roots on, let them
dangle

And the dirt

Just to make clear
where they come from

– Charles Olsen

We don't enter into the world; we come out of it. The earth sings. When we hear it, we rise up singing our own deep song. It is like an energy welling up from some basic force beneath our feet, an elemental force that gives us our words and rekindles our world with a warmth from the inside. The unleashing of transformative ideas will not be prescribed from above; it will be a welling up from below.

If there is to be a common understanding regarding how the 'unsolid' matter of place fits together, it will come to us through art and from our own deep song. We need to leave the roots and dirt on our thoughts and words just to remind ourselves where they came from. Too often we sanitize our words and the deep truth contained in them.

Instead, our work is to let the soul speak through us in ways that are unvarnished so this basic force may flow through us and into the world again.

In our rush to become smarter, more efficient and more rational, we have allowed the deep song to atrophy. Life fills us from the inside. When we forget this, we often don't know what is welling up from the inside and compelling us to do what we do. Deep song awakens it again. Deep song is the music of simple genuine mystery, of deep questions, of inner truth, of yearning and sorrow, of ecstasy and music filled with feeling and emotion.

Deep song is born floating on the wind. It is the natural music of the woods and the streams. It is music with deep roots in the countryside. It is heard in folk melodies and in the yearning to be reunited with the soul of place again.

Music critic Tom Huizenga writes about listening to American mezzo soprano Joyce DiDonato in the role of Mary Queen of Scots one evening at the Metropolitan Opera in New York. "I knew she would be good," he wrote, "but I wasn't prepared for what came to me as she sang her aria."

> DiDonato's voice — so luminous, so expressive, so technically assured — entered my ears as if it were some kind of drug. I was immediately in tears — not tears of sadness but of awestruck euphoria. And then, she pared her voice down to a tiny, shining thread... that

pure, hushed tone was all you could hear as DiDonato
held nearly 4,000 people in the palm of her hand.
(Huizenga, NPR January 2013.)

Anything that fills us from the inside is our deep song.

We cannot find a new balance by looking for it in all the familiar
absolutes such as machines or economies or technology. The song
that calls us into the future arises unprompted from nature, from
art, from spontaneous speech and from our communal life together.
It springs forth from the authentic expression of our own luminous
nature — bursting forth from beneath. It is the source of nourishment that bubbles up from below that makes us rich and makes us
full.

For Spanish poet Garcia Lorca, the sound that Tom Huizenga heard
that evening was the *duende,* a sound so arresting and ancient and
true that we will listen for it again and again.

The duende is the true expression of the prophetic spirit that lies
in the dark soil beneath our feet. It is heard in music and song, in
nature, in art and in community. It is seen in dance and in Carnival.
It is the gift of our own true self, arousing our hearts through the
prophetic voice and spoken word.

Duende connects us to the source of authentic and emotional
expression. It brings about a sudden uplifting of the spirit and a
fresh viewpoint as expressed through the spontaneous re-ordering or
changing of structure and form.

While we may look above for spirit and inspiration, it is the soulful
spirit of the duende in art and in spontaneous speech and action
that is the deep source of aliveness within us.

In this sense, the duende, instead of offering an explanation,
expresses a vision that propels us into a dream of a future reuniting

us with our hopes from the past. It is a power and a force rather than an abstraction or a thought. We hear its power expressed in the words of an old maestro of the guitar when he says, "The duende is not in the throat; the duende climbs up inside you from the soles of your feet. The duende is from a true living style of blood, of the most ancient culture, of spontaneous creation." (Lorca, 1955.)

This also goes to the heart of Carnival. It is not just a skill, show or display, but an engagement with the vital force of life itself. This distinction is essential for understanding the roots of deep song and the Carnival spirit.

Accessing this generative power of duende is not something we can specifically *do*. We cannot grasp or possess or own it. Instead, it is a gift and a knowingness that finds its edges — as Lorca would speak of it — in the remotest regions of our inner life.

When the root system isn't healthy, the tree is not being nourished and over time will die. This happens when the fundamental generative forces within our organization, community and ourselves are not flourishing. When there is no depth, there is no soul. Without soul, our art and our actions in the world are lifeless.

When there is not an authentic life, and we have no true place to act from, the health of the larger system suffers as well. The deep work Lorca writes of is an unleashing of this generative force, a force that is not remote from us but, instead, has its roots in our own authentic nature.

To embrace duende is to also embrace an alternative future. In a rule-bound world where there is suspicion about the unpredictable nature of the duende and the felt life, acts of Carnival through ritual, pause and celebration, art and dialogue bring it to life again. It brings us home to the presence of places and wisdom of our own local traditions and identity, to a renewal of our life in art and a commitment to the work of craft as a vocation and public practice.

In Carnival, it is not the managers or the professionals but the poets, the artists and the prophets who welcome us into this new world. It is the poet/leader who says the world we seek is already within us. We *are* nature, we are soil, we are the music and the poem — what ripens in the soil also burns in our blood. What is out there in the larger world is also alive in us as well.

If, in the hierarchical world, the story always ends in death, in Carnival it ends in a banquet. As we saw in the story of Mabelle Park, the transformation from urban scrubland to a place of magic was curated through brick ovens and feasts. This festive nature of Carnival is reflected in the feasting and breaking of the bread together.

Convening public gatherings with a meal is the most common form for introducing a cycle of initiation toward a new awakening. The acts of tasting, savouring, swallowing and digesting are the festive forms of nourishment and symbols of transformation. We don't just listen to words; we chew on and savour them — words good enough to be eaten, words that can nourish the birth of new ideas, are at the root of the festive spirit.

WHEREVER YOU STAND:

BEING TRUE TO OUR OWN NATURE

What makes a place a place is its soul — and with this the realization that in that place we cannot be anything other than ourselves.

What is most apparent in Carnival is laughter. Laughter offers the perspective of liberation, the loosening of limitations and the spontaneous expression of the collective body. It comes from the idea of the poet, the musician/artist, the fool, the magician, the jester, the disruptive stranger — the ones who represent and speak to the dominance of economic absolutes from the perspective of our shared sense of place and the common life we share. And what releases this gaiety of spirit is the realization that to be true to the soul in our own lives is not something we need to specifically do, but to be. And to be true to the jester spirit is to celebrate being fully and truly ourselves.

The jester is the one who asserts the sanctity of our place in the world and bears witness against the dominance of those whose appetites are to consume it.

American poet Raymond Carver beautifully portrays the life force of the jester spirit of duende in his poem "The Juggler at Heaven's Gate." (Carver, 2000.)

…How'd he get in the act, anyway? What's his story?
That's the story I want to know. Anybody
can wear a gun and swagger around. Or fall in love
with somebody who loves somebody else. But to juggle
for God's sake! To give your life to that.
To go with that. Juggling.

"That's the story I want to know," Carver writes.

With these words, he transforms a dusty street in Sweetwater, Wyoming, into a place where, if just for a moment, the Carnival spirit of the jester's world brings the main street to a standstill.

"What's his story?" the man looking through the grimy hotel window asks. By an "amazing act of the mind and hands," the juggler crafts something of significance and beauty — something unrepeatable — that transforms the sense of place forever.

The irony is that, in this land of gunfighters and mavericks, this juggler is the real outlaw. By standing in the centre of his own art, as if he belonged there and nowhere else, this juggler is the one living outside the rules. This sense of feeling at home with oneself, including being honest with ourselves regarding where home is, is our first step. When we have courageously taken this step, life steps in and takes all the rest.

In contrast, the dominant economic order seeks not spontaneous expression, but closure. To rest in playful uncertainty is alien to a mind that imagines comfort can be found only in the search for completion through restless, constant productivity. This is in sharp contrast to the careful attention and wisdom of the work of craft. The artist, the designer and the poet are the ones who throw off the old order to remake places that remain true to our inner song and our own true nature.

"Can you hear it?" the craftsperson asks. In reclaiming the story of deep song and our own poetic spirit, we may hear again the yearning to reconnect with the soul of the world.

> At every moment, he works close to a boundary, an invisible wall that defines the path to the next moment that moves ahead of him as he follows it, a wall that he never quite touches. Patience in the craftsman is the willingness to recognize and obey the movement of this wall.

> "Can you hear it?" he asks; it is the sound of the edge moving into the wood, of the mallet descending, of the thin slip of the shuttle, of the fingers on clay. (Remde, 1985.)

Can You Hear It?

Placemaking and the Democratic Imagination

The public square has always been the cradle for spontaneous out-bursts of the popular will. But what we are hearing now is both more continuous and more coherent, signifying the return of the poet singing the deep song of democracy, a melody rich in promise, as we re-imagine our place in the emergence of civil society on a global scale.

Historically the place where this collective consciousness forms is the public square. For many the public square has atrophied, an anachronism from times long past. But in times of rapid expansion and uncertainty, we have to make our communities wherever we find them. The public square is where we gather when we cannot find another place.

"Can you hear it?" the artist asks.

When we hear this, our song at birth, we remember that we are all in essence members of a community — a circle of gifts — gathered together by our common love of place. We live for place. And when things are not right in the world — when our sense of place has been silenced, when there is no place for our gift and our craft can't find an outward expression in the world — it is in the nature of Carnival and the jester spirit to come together to reclaim our place in the world. It rises up with a groundswell of creative energy and reclaims the commons and the public square, where we may be seen for who we truly are and where our stories can be heard once again.

Such places as Tahir Square in Cairo, Taksim Square in Istanbul, Place de la Bastille in Paris, Tiananmen Square in Beijing, Wenceslas Square in Prague, Mohammad Bouazizi Square in Tunisia, Independence Square in Kyiv, as well as large-scale social movements — Arab Spring, Quebec Autumn, Idle No More, the Occupy movement — are growing deep networks of connection and influencing the social agenda in ways that are not yet fully understood.

These squares and the cities they inhabit are older than most countries. For hundreds of years they have stood at the nexus where people have gathered to remind governments that they are not only consumers and taxpayers but citizens who intend to write new collective narratives for their future. It is these streets and squares where we are witnessing the emerging of a global soul and with this the re-energizing of a form of speaking that is not based on making announcements or lecturing, but on revealing new truths and possibilities in a prophetic way.

"Let the healing begin," Auden writes. "And teach a new man to praise." The healing begins by co-creating moments of collective transcendence that disrupt the status quo and in which we experience what it means to be a part of something larger than ourselves and at the same time where we can discover what is most natural within ourselves. Not all social movements advocate tolerance and diversity of thought — too often they are intended to replace one singular ideology with another — but where there is tolerance, goodwill, diversity of thought and the spirit of art, the voices we hear may be our future destiny re-imagining itself through us. "Can you hear it?" the artist asks. In the cacophony of voices around us we need to listen deeply to hear what we are being called to do.

What we are hearing is the call for a new beginning. We stand now on the threshold of a historic shift. Leadership is happening, but it is not coming from the traditional institutions any longer.. In this new story, it will not be the institutions but the community itself that will be our consolation. We will hear the soul of place speaking to us through the invisible architecture of talking circles, public gatherings, global crowd sourcing and national conversations. The future is arriving with the extraordinary generation of new initiatives, but these innovations are not coming from above. They are rising up like the duende in the form of a great wellspring from beneath our feet.

In the autumn of 2011, 7,000 people calling themselves Occupy Wall Street 'walked the forest together' as they appeared on Manhattan's Zuccotti Park in New York City. They overflowed onto the corners and sidewalks. They had heard the call. For a time the Occupy movement, despite its disorganized feel and disruptive jester spirit, filled and transformed the public square. Many of the basics — portable toilets, nutritious local food, medical tents, a protocol for consensus and innovations such as the people's microphone — mysteriously appeared. At its peak, this movement inspired many thousands more to not only demonstrate but to express diverse grievances and concern for the future of the world.

Artists and craftspeople are familiar with how Carnival and the spirit of deep song transform public places through intense elevations of mood and compelling moments of inspired creation. These are prophetic moments, wellsprings of feeling, when we experience the prophetic sense that we are *being* played, *being* spoken, *being* moved to action or *being* led to articulate a destiny for our future that builds upon what we most treasure from our past.

The Occupy movement signalled one of those transformative shifts. It spoke of a resurgence of the spirit of democracy and the expression of a public will toward the remaking of our places by restoring the vibrant spontaneity of the public square.

In this spirit, thousands came together around the world, not for a sports event or rock concert — which have served as common outlets for this groundswell of transcendent feeling — but to let their hearts be healed by singing songs of praise, songs that expressed the desire for a rebirth of the democratic spirit and to shape a dream of the future in a new and compelling way.

This dream included redefining our public role from being consumers to being co-creators. In the spirit of Carnival, this points toward throwing off the dominance and absolutism of the prevailing economic order. In its place we were seeing a movement toward a new relationship with creation, with the land and with placemaking as the new absolutes. If we are to have a positive future, economics must serve a higher purpose, one based on deepening the soul of a regenerative and spiritual economy with which we can align our gifts and which is place-based.

While such movements will ebb and flow as all creative cycles do, what is significant is that, at least in the early stages, the Occupy movement was marked by the healing of the heart and the liberation of the human spirit through deep songs of praise as expressed through dance, music, art, ceremony, conversation and story. We see how the seeds of transformative change often start as we witness people walking, hugging, laughing, crying and being moved and transformed in the company of one another. The Occupy movement may be a footnote in history now, but as nation states become archaic — too big to solve some problems and too small to solve others — cities and public squares are on the rise, setting the ground for other gatherings to arise like a wave anywhere and at any time.

"Can you hear it?" the artist asks. When we work close to the boundary and when the only sound is the edge moving into the wood, we hear, embedded in the chaos of the world, the expression of our own deep song. This song is sung by whoever most serves the moment with words that facilitate a coming together of the whole.

This trust in expressing our own deep song is a rare achievement; to risk speaking without knowing in advance what we will say reaches beyond the certainties of thinking and planning that usually power our public voice.

This form of speaking invites a depth of yearning and desire the analytic voice does not generally allow or accept. The prophetic voice is moved to speak in a way that transforms individual sentiment into a communal experience through words of praise that awaken the heart and make hope possible.

"Who is it now that speaks for the whole?" we ask. While the old story was given to us, the new story is one we give to ourselves. It will become a tapestry created out of the many threads offered by whoever is moved in that moment to speak.

"We didn't come to plan; we came to talk," one Occupier said. And this may be what signalled the significance of the movement. It was not a protest or a demonstration or a march. Rather, it was an assembly — a commons, a carnival, a leaderless group intent upon opening a door to a world of possibility we may not have imagined before.

The spirited, friendly and optimistic Occupy gathering in Toronto (which paralleled the gathering in New York) suggested this was a new kind of social phenomenon. While there were diverse ideas about what the gatherings would achieve, that was not what really mattered. Participants' focus seemed not to have been on a cohesive goal but instead to serve as prophets of a possible future by talking about what those goals could be.

The core questions of the movement seemed to be: are we on the right path? And what kind of place do we want to create?

Some dismissed the Occupy movement as insignificant because it lacked clear goals; this may reflect frustrated questions coming from the old story trying to make sense of the new.

The movement seemed to be addressing something else, something beyond the constraints of goals and outcomes and more akin to a collective search for a creative synthesis to alleviate the sense of life-lessness in our public realm.

We all carry within our own heart the deep song and prophetic voice of duende that speaks for the whole. The new beginnings of our communal life are not orchestrated by one person but manifested through conversations with the whole of the community. In conversation, we do not speak in a formal way. Instead we are moved to speech by ancient forces that re-ignite humanity's passion, the capacity for mutual care and the commitment to create a place for the healing of the heart in the world.

In this context, if the Occupy story was simply an economic protest, it would have been even more short-lived. If it was a summons to come together as a healing force to re-enliven our place in the larger world, what we were hearing may have been much more profound. Unlike the average protest, where people are abstractions to a higher singular ideology, the Occupy movement began as an assembly — as in the popular weekly assemblies in Spain that emerged not just in cities but in neighbourhoods around the country — that promised a discussion without fixating on a particular issue, person or ideology. True to the spontaneous spirit of the duende, which also had its roots in the Andalusia region of Spain, no one anticipated that the evolving, global, many-months-long assemblies would emerge out of those first days of Occupy Wall Street and affect change on a broader scale.

Speaking Out:

The Prophetic Power of Voice

While the prophetic voice of the poet/artist is often overshadowed by the formidable power of established authority, this formal authority doesn't know Carnival. In a world out of balance, ultimately it is this jester spirit and the arts that transforms the public square into an apex for transformative change through reigniting our hunger to re-embrace the power of place and the mythic imagination.

In the recent ferment of movements that are creating fundamental shifts in how we see our place in the world, this prophetic voice has been exercised in several ways.

1. Those who came spoke with no official standing other than from the wisdom of their heart and the places they came from. They drew their wisdom to speak from the authority of their own felt life rather than from a defined and detailed strategy or ideology worked out in advance.

2. They engaged the public square with the imaginative and playful sense of creation itself. They presented their case not through formal briefs, studies or reports but through the invitational power of Carnival embodied in stories, music, dance, drumming and song.

3. They offered the world a narrative of hope, basing their vision

on how the future might be made right rather than only on what is wrong with it. The strength of the prophetic voice is that it is a voice of promise and not despair. It is the intuitive voice that senses and articulates the future before it happens.

4. The narrative is shared in the form of a vision of the future rather than an explanation. The purpose of poetry — as with all art — is to experience rather than explain. The voice of the poet/artist invites the listener to re-imagine with them the nature of the common life we want to share together.

5. The prophetic voice is clarified through ferment and adversity, not weakened by it. As philosopher Paul Valery wrote, "A person is a poet if his imagination is stimulated by the difficulties inherent in his art and not if his imagination is dulled by them. As such the poet speaks out of the ferment of social upheaval, not from above it."

The idea that we speak out of the ferment of the place itself and not from above is the foundation for placemaking. As the Occupy conversations unfolded on the street and in the camps, people who had grieved the sense of dislocation and loss of place in a competitive and isolating world were finding their voice, and with this a new sense of community — a culture of possibility — that was inclusive, respectful, supportive and, most importantly, horizontal.

This movement toward shifting the architecture from vertical to horizontal structures would mark the most significant change in rethinking how we make our place in the world. Insights regarding placemaking will come from these diverse ideas and possibilities overlapping, blending and coexisting in a common field.

By having created this fundamental shift, even for a short time, the Occupy story may have accomplished something that could change everything. It has tilled the soil for a new national conversation. It has achieved this by recognizing that, at a time when the old story is no longer adequate and the new story is not yet here, we were witnessing the seeds of a new narrative, one that brought many minds together to think collectively and horizontally about the larger global challenges diminishing our sense of place.

Earlier, I described the image of dark clouds resulting from the uprooting of the grasslands of the American plains. The Occupy movement warned of another threat: the roots of community being ploughed under by economic and market forces turning members of the public into consumers and taxpayers, denying them their rights of participation and citizenship.

Many who came to the public gatherings expressed frustration and bewilderment. They felt disengaged from one another and strangers to their own sense of place. They found themselves caught up in a whirlwind of impersonal and technological activities that characterize the restless productivity of our time. Few had the time to attend to the delicate fabric of relationships that make up the substrata of community.

The roots of community, like the prairie grasses themselves, are small, lattice-like structures of informal, social, cultural and ecological relationships decentralizing economic and political power. Just as the prairie wasn't composed of one grass, these delicate, local relationships — whether they involve small entrepreneurial businesses, associations, craft guilds, schools, town committees, roundtables, neighbourhoods, volunteer activities including civic, religious or fraternal organizations — serve as the vital connectors that keep the topsoil of our communities from blowing away. The life and health of the commons depends on their interconnectedness. The risk is that they are often seen as soft assets and thus expendable when the pressure arises to save rather than to invest or spend.

The bulwark that protects us from the wind is conversation, particularly about our stories, our aspirations, our roots, and the significance and challenges regarding the uniqueness of the place we share. Conversations are not just options for spending idle time together; they are necessary because they are about values and what is important. They moisten the roots and build the soil so that, when a crisis arises, the ground has been prepared for responding quickly, wisely and collectively.

The Occupy movement was criticized for lacking an organized voice. Perhaps this is because we have lost our collective voice. Our language is in decline, taken over by professional groups who speak in code in an increasingly specialized and placeless society.

The industrial and technological ages did not place a high value on language-making. Metaphors drawn from computers, sports, war and machines are often composed not in complete sentences but in data and bits — or code. This code is a defence from authenticity and leaves us ill-equipped and speechless when the time comes to grapple with larger, complex questions regarding ethics, values, emotional challenges and larger meanings.

If there is a hunger in the land, perhaps it is the hunger to speak not in code or sound bites but in complete sentences again.

In ancient times, the purpose of language was not only to inform but to transform. Our words reflected the range and depth of our shared experience of place. Time in nature, art and craftwork, literature and community and art were but a few places we could go to find the roots of language-making. Now, Paul Hawken writes, the average person has learned to recognize more than 1,000 corporate logos but can recognize fewer than 10 plants and animals native to their own locality (Hawken, 1993).

The pace of our lives inhibits our ability to take the time to express what we really mean, to immerse ourselves in the spaces and places that root our language in experiences that feel real. We often don't create the time and place to engage in the complex transformational conversations needed for us to be effective stewards of the place we occupy in a changeable and chaotic world.

In the absence of the front porch, our leaders talk in voices that seem lifeless and in a language disembodied from their experiences and felt life. This leads to a struggle to recover the lost craft of authentic speech and to articulate intelligently and passionately about the things that deeply matter to us.

So while the Occupy movement was about many things, including economic disparities, social justice and public spaces, it was also about re-asserting our power to co-create transcendent moments together. To those who discredit the movement, complaining that the process was cumbersome and slow and it had no voice, others, like Jay Gaussoin, a 46-year-old unemployed carpenter and craftsman who was finding his public voice through the movement, said in reply, "But so is democracy. We're so distracted these days, people have forgotten how to focus. But the 'mic check' demands not just that we listen to other people's opinions but that we really hear what they're saying, because we have to repeat their words exactly… It requires an architecture of consciousness" — an apt phrase, as Michael Kimmelman noted in his 2011 *New York Times* piece on Occupy Wall Street.

A LUMINOUS GROUND:

IGNITING MANY POINTS OF LIGHT

One thing we may have learned regarding the sustainability of transformational change is that it will not be vertical but horizontal. Creating a positive future will involve partnering with many points of light in the world.

Several years have passed since the height of the Occupy movement. Following its first anniversary it had all but disappeared. Though many of the ingredients that first fed the movement are just as evident today, the coalition may have felt it had achieved its goal. Whether that's true or not, the Occupy movement has largely faded from national headlines and apparently been sapped of its initial public support.

What happened, and why did it fade from view?

Perhaps this scenario that unfolded on a London street may offer an explanation:

> At the Occupy movement in London, outside St. Paul's Cathedral, an older, middle-class woman looking at the grungy tents asked me: What are they accomplishing? But if there'd been an assembly in her own neighbourhood, she might have gone and felt less perplexed;

'they' might even have asked her what she'd like to accomplish. (Salutin, *Toronto Star* 2012.)

However justified the means behind the Occupy movement's goals, over time and following the initial euphoric sense that this was something new, it became apparent that the focus was more on scarcity and grievance than on abundance, hope and possibility.

It is one thing to hear the deep song; it is another to discern its subtle meaning and follow its call.

Shifting the focus to grievance and scarcity, however justified, eventually triggers a cycle of anxiety and despair that leads to anger, fear and aggression. It is difficult to hold a negative vision and expect a positive result. This may explain how it was that the Occupy camps shifted from being gathering places of conversation to fortresses of resistance and opposition that had to be defended as the risk of violence both within and outside the camps increased.

In the Assemblies in Spain, a different scenario unfolded. Where the Occupy movement congregated in centralized camps in the public square, the Spanish Assemblies met in local neighbourhoods, creating multiple 'public squares' around the country. In other words, wherever there had been a camp in Spain there was now an assembly. This differentiated them from North America's Occupy movements, which set up camps and clung stubbornly to them, as though they were guerrilla strongholds, waiting to be evicted and vowing to move back.

And the principle of life that is at work and contributes to the art of assembly is that, for wholeness to emerge, we need not only one centre but many centres, each emerging in ways unique and distinct in relation to all the rest. What appears then is an elegant latticework of centres each rooted to itself and at the same time connected to the whole. The essential features of these centres are their uniqueness and originality and that they are not specific to human communities but also include the more-than-human world as well. As architect Christopher Alexander writes in his book *The Nature of Order* (2002), even the apple leaf in the apple orchard occurs in a field of centres. This is the basis for a living structure and the luminous ground to which we all belong.

So in Spain — and this is perhaps one example among many others — each centre exists within a living web of connection to other centres. This generative creation of multiple centres, where each grows in resilience in the presence of all the rest, enabled a shift from organizing resistance through staged events and public occupations to convening meetings in neighbourhoods that engaged locals who had never been involved in public conversations before. It did so not so much through the impersonal strategies of social media — because many who came were not on the Internet — but by designating public spaces as gathering places through invitational strategies such as neighbourhood posters and word of mouth.

"If there was pressure to move, the Assemblies would disband voluntarily and move to other neighbourhoods. In other words, where the Occupy Movement resisted opposition until forced to disperse, the Assemblies simply 'dissolved in order to expand,'" said Salutin (*Toronto Star*, 2012).

And where the Occupy movement tended to coalesce around one idea and one voice — "We are the 99 percent" — the Spanish Assemblies welcomed multiple voices and perspectives. This created a place for multiple ideologies to be present without any one point of view dominating. They created a petition with not just one message but six separate points — something that echoes the Native American practice of the Rule of Six.

With the Native tradition of the Rule of Six, the conversation seeks to expand the possible theories or perspectives we might hold about a particular event. When we have six ways of thinking about a problem or issue, it is possible to move forward in ways that do not create unnecessary opposition or tension. When we see something from six different points of view, we generate more data and naturally create an environment of abundance and possibility rather than one of scarcity.

In contrast to the Occupy movement, which had a rule of one, which was to oppose institutional life and reject political parties and the electoral process, the assemblies' goal was to integrate the gatherings into the political process in order to blend with them. They did so by working toward a consensus whereby popular ideas built upon through dialogue were forwarded to higher assemblies and potentially integrated into the political process. In this respect the assemblies were not focused on dismantling the electoral process but on adding a layer in the space between so that citizens could influence the political process between elections.

Also unlike the Occupy sites, which became staged events or spectacles that often overlooked the normal day-to-day activities, the assemblies were integrated into the everyday life of the community. Where Occupy sites tended to exclude normal activity when they took over a park or street and you needed to be a "member" to attend, the assemblies became an integral part of the life of the street. There might have been a mariachi band or a circus or carnival as well as hawkers and other forms of bustling activity; assemblies were not in conflict with their adversaries but rather created an atmosphere of inclusiveness in which all were welcomed. In essence, where the Occupy movement said, "Join us," the assemblies said, "We will join you." (Ibid, 2010.)

What may have started with music, conversations and prophetic speech in the Occupy movement became formal speeches and platforms. In the assemblies they had dialogue. The assemblies didn't want to convince anyone what was right or wrong; they wanted to get people talking. They had learned a difficult cultural lesson:

radical action does not necessarily lead to change. Nor does the institutional order need to break down for significant and meaningful change to occur.

Through creating multiple spaces for public discourse, the assemblies were honouring the soul of place. They became an integral part of street life and created forms of public engagement where joyful celebration and spontaneous duende — like groundswells of feeling and action — were possible. They tried to take the resentment people felt about inequality and transform it not into aggressive action but into an abundance of ideas through collective discourse so that coherent action could occur.

And because the assemblies were not planned but arose spontaneously, out of a spirit of celebration itself, they took root in neighbourhoods as a natural and organic expression of the people's will. Even skeptics felt they witnessed something genuine as people sat in circles with no agenda and no attempt at overt control. It was a real assembly.

In engaging in this way the people were also returning to their roots. The assemblies had been an integral part of public life in Spain for centuries. This was the case in other parts of the world as well.

The assemblies have made people free and therefore served as one of the oldest forms of place and placemaking. This public commons embodies the spirit of embracing local traditions, which has been an integral aspect of meetings in public life from ancient times in Athens to New England's town halls to neighbourhood learning centres in churches, schools and local shopping malls. (11)

Moments of Turning:

Creating Cultures of Regenerativity

*The primary work of the next century will be
learning how to regenerate living systems*

– Charles Krone

At the core of our existence is a pool of energy that has very little to do with personal identity. From this common pool of energy, the music plays itself and the painting paints itself. This is the world of regenerativity, a world in which we play only a small part in the whole marvellous act of creation.

The global challenge now is to cultivate the conditions where life is free to generate and create new life. In a regenerative world, creation creates itself. This involves turning from a linear and closely controlled environment to a more integrative and holistic worldview.

The global call to gather together and engage in pubic discourse signals the groundswell for the cultural shifts to come. The shifts will be regenerative as we discover how to not only sustain life but to create life out of whatever resources, gifts and talents are available to us.

It is a time when linear, narrow approaches that have carved our world into grids and straight lines will give way to new images such as circles and spirals that are more holistic, integrative and life-affirming.

Several principles may guide this metamorphosis and our advance toward creating a more resilient and livable world:

1. NURTURING THE SHARING OF GIFTS

Every place is a microcosm of the future, and it is through our gifts that we invite that future in. Everyone has a gift; the act of seeing the gift in the other lies at the heart of creating a regenerative life. Unlike our skills and abilities, which are acquired, our gifts are bestowed. Our gifts connect us to a deep well of intuitive wisdom, which is at the root of the life force itself. And as the gift is passed along, it acquires new layers of meaning and significance. To thrive, the gift needs to stay in circulation. It represents the currency of abundance. As such it is through the process of gift-sharing that we create the conditions for a regenerativity culture where the gift is called out and life can thrive.

2. ENCOURAGING UNBRIDLED OPTIMISM

Creating a culture of regenerativity is based on nurturing the life-affirming power of gifts, hope and possibility. In this context, deepening our awareness of different places includes seeing what is possible within them. This unbridled optimism stands in contrast to our prevailing attitudes, which often arise as a consequence of being separated from place, heightening our focus on problems, needs and deficiencies. When we don't know where we come from or where we belong — and our larger cultural narrative of place is unclear — we may be mistrustful toward life. So, nurturing a more optimistic and regenerative worldview begins with creating new and vibrant narratives of place to which everyone can belong. When our sense of place is made more clear, we can let go of our preoccupation with taking action to close gaps and instead reflect on how to tap into and manifest our innate potential for generating new opportunities for creativity and innovation.

3. Embracing the Soul of Carnival

Whenever we create places for people to become more whole, we are invoking the spirit of Carnival. Carnival is an event. It is also a state of being — celebrating the whole of life, including its darker tones. Carnival is the expression of the poetic spirit that clears away the old order to open the space for the regenerative force of life to flow through. As such, Carnival raises our spirits, awakens our senses and helps us see and act in new ways. Where in one moment there was nothing, now there is something. As the advocate for embracing the fullness of life, this is the poetic mystery of Carnival. Canadian poet Don McKay writes, "The poetic frame permits the possible to be experienced as a power rather than a deficiency; it permits the imagination entry, finding wider resonances, leading us to contemplate further implications for ourselves." (McKay, 2011.)

Carnival can also be enacted through small gestures. For example, in a recent community conversation, we did several things that embraced the spirit of playfulness, ceremony and celebration that honoured the sense of occasion we were experiencing. To begin we brought the language of beauty into the centre of our work. We did so by bringing live music into the room to help with moments of transition and to deepen pauses for reflection. We did it by sharing stories of a time when we had experienced the beauty of the human spirit in moments of crisis, and we did it by inviting silence as each stepped outside in nature to find something they could bring back and add to the centrepiece that would invite our harvest reflections for the day.

There are many ways we celebrate the wholeness of Carnival through art, silence, movement and reflection. Together they set the stage for a language of regenerativity to unfold.

4. Crafting a Language of Life

A language of place is a language of life. Consultant Peter Block says that "all transformation is linguistic." The art of oratory involves knowing the place we speak from so we may give back to language the nobility of voice and the authority of the spoken word. Words create worlds, and the limits of our language are the limits of our world. Language also helps us see. When we speak of beauty and aliveness, we see and experience more beauty and aliveness. They are invisible until we speak their names. Creating a regenerative culture includes creating a language with which to describe and experience it. A language of life therefore is also a language of relationship, a living language that is deeply rooted in those places most full of life, including the work of craft, of nature and living systems, of community and our common life together. In this context the art of oratory is embodied in whoever is committed to the art of speaking on behalf of the whole. Even more, it is found in the one who, in the chosen moment, can initiate others to even greater levels of understanding and awareness by speaking the unspoken and, in so doing, serve as the vehicle for expressing the unanimous voice of the whole.

A language of life draws from a vocabulary that connects us to the wonderment of life through such words as unfoldment, companionship, connection, touch, beauty, love, harmony, resilience and enchantment. These are words that align with the natural forces of life in contrast to the more common use of a linear vocabulary that implies life is our adversary against whose natural forces we must work in order to achieve our goals. Common words like targets, impact, leverage, force, evidence, pressure, acceleration, breakthrough and speed, when examined more closely for the tone they set, may have this unintended effect.

5. Creating Place in a Beautiful Way

To be regenerative is to walk in beauty and to fill a place in a beautiful way. The word beauty itself is closely related to both calling and compassion. As such, beauty lies at the root of what it means to be truly compassionate and truly alive. It is our call to life. Ultimately it will be the beauty of the human spirit that will guide us toward a more regenerative and compassionate world. The power of beauty is that it stands at the threshold of the visible and the invisible world. Seeing the world as beautiful helps us see patterns, connections and relationships often invisible to the untrained eye. To be regenerative is to return the world to beauty.

6. Celebrating Art as Invitation

Art will be central in growing a regenerative culture and brings our humanity into the room — particularly art that is offered not as a performance or entertainment but as the expression of hospitality, inclusiveness, diversity and generosity.

Art invites empathy and shared understanding. It invites memorable stories and powerful metaphors. As such, art points us to places in our experience where words cannot go. Art offers the integration of the mind with the heart and the body. Through our art we can be vulnerable with one another and create bridges to unite whatever has divided us.

7. Welcoming the Stranger

Art can also be disruptive. The artist is often the outsider, the powerful stranger who poses the unanswerable questions. Welcoming the stranger into our midst is the most direct way of acknowledging and respecting our own — and each other's — vulnerability in the great mystery of what is to come. In the face of the unknown we need to resist the comforting temptation to retreat behind the walls with our own tribe and instead invite others in who may see differently. This offers a place for the outliers — the rebels, dreamers, amateurs, elders, youth, and aboriginal cultures — who often find themselves voiceless and vulnerable in times of uncertainty and disruptive change.

8. TELLING OUR STORIES

To be good storytellers also requires us to be good story listeners and story catchers. Storytelling is not a performance but an act of intimate reciprocity. In this reciprocity, we create a bond with another. Stories introduce emotion into our conversations. Stories also encourage an open and curious mind and nurture a spirit of joy and delight. Every aspect of our experience can be held in story. As such, stories are integral to the great transitions and changes that are before us, including storytellers and artists in the midst of new initiatives and the dissemination of new ideas. And because stories are one of the primary tools the jester has of telling truth to power, stories hold the power to shift our culture away from blame, mistrust and fault-finding toward greater learning, openness and trust.

9. CURATING A CULTURE OF PUBLIC DISCOURSE

The Occupy movement, Idle No More and other movements signal the profound and largely unmet appetite among many to bring their voice to local and global governance. These gatherings represent the wave of the future. Every voice matters, and these voices can be heard most clearly when we advocate for environments that foster trust and integrity, interdependence across diverse disciplines, civic engagement, transparency and openness. When the public is seen primarily through the narrow lens of their role as consumers and taxpayers rather than as citizens and contributors to the commons and collective will of the public good, the actions of institutions will lead to suppressing life rather than regenerating it. There is now, emerging in the populace, a hunger to participate in public discourse and placemaking. This desire for engagement will also contribute to building the social capital so that, when a crisis does arise, the community has nourished the collective will and beauty of the human spirit to cope with it.

10. IGNITING MANY POINTS OF LIGHT

We need to retrain the eye to see the world not in silos but as living systems that are seamless, organic and collaborative. Regenerative cultures are not hierarchical but horizontal. They are represented by broad-based and diverse networks of connection — many points of light — that create dynamic and fluid social fields for learning and co-generation. The intersections between, within and across these social fields allow for the changeable clustering and regrouping of creative forces so that the vein of gold that animates human effort is always fully engaged.

Creative initiative is often stifled not because of personal deficiency but because the structures are not closely aligned with the work required. Just as musicians need instruments that match their talent, we need to be aware of how the design of places itself enables and supports, even augments, the free flow of energy needed to accomplish the work at hand. Whether these points of light are workgroups, roundtables, neighbourhoods, cities or global networks, a deep understanding of how we design structures that contribute activities and solutions that are systemic, participative and insightful will be needed.

11. RE-IMAGINING OUR MYTHIC LIFE TOGETHER

We need renewed myths, symbols and metaphors to express what cannot be spoken of literally. The power of metaphor is that it is provisional. A metaphor does not present black-and-white answers but, rather, alternative perspectives from which we may choose those that feel most alive and intriguing to us.

A provisional metaphoric world also embraces the notion that life creates life. This lies at the heart of every mythic story and draws us to the greater story of humanity and the mystery of what it means to be fully human and fully alive. Many of the challenges we confront today are a result of being disconnected from this larger mythic narrative. Without appropriate myths, legends and stories to help set the larger context for our work and lift us up into the 'realm of the muses,' the potential of our personal and community stories cannot be fully realized.

To engage the mythic life is to undertake the timeless journey toward exploring our personal and collective life together through the four archetypal stories: The Sovereign, The Weaver, The Enchanter and The Steward. Whatever their name, they represent the four directions of change and hold the key to awakening us to our own inner life. As such the mythic life involves a journey across many landscapes of place, each offering ancient wisdom on how to live and evolve together.

TOWARD A NEW
LIGHTNESS OF BEING:

THE METAMORPHOSIS OF PLACE

In the life of the cells we are all artists 'living on the edge,' ready to be transformed in an instant.

From local sharing circles to national conversations to global 'crowdsourcing' where millions of people, young and old, can mobilize together to engage complex issues and build a new society on a scale of collaboration never seen before — all of these initiatives give reason for optimism in the human community's capacity to reinvent itself and recover the soul of place again.

Creating a regenerative world includes invoking feelings of curiosity, joy, flexibility and delight — feelings that contribute toward a lightness of being that leads to the metamorphosis of any place we happen to be.

When we practice these principles of regenerativity we also stimulate, in a metaphoric way, the growth of new cellular structures, which could be described as imaginal cells. The pattern of these imaginal cells, or discs, as they were referred to when they were first researched in the context of insect development by Dutch biologist Jan Swammerdam in the 1600s, has been described more recently by Norrie Huddle in her book *Butterfly*.

Imaginal cells are temporary cells that activate the process of the caterpillar's metamorphosis within the chrysalis to butterfly. They also serve as a powerful metaphor for humankind's evolutionary leap forward. They awaken the imagination to a mythic story of how the power of our collective intelligence can create new possibilities for a positive future.

Norrie Huddle writes, "Then at some point, the entire string of imaginal cells suddenly realize all together that it is something different from the caterpillar. Something New! Something Wonderful! ...and that realization is the shout of the birth of the butterfly!" (Huddle, 1990.)

In this context, words matter. They hold the power to create new cells that imagine new stories and create new worlds. Just as imaginal cells in the caterpillar first form in clumps that gradually join together, collaborating through dialogue, assemblies and public gatherings germinates imaginal cells that awaken the heart to mythic possibilities and a larger story of our place in the world that is ripe with meaning and possibility.

Imaginal cells change our physiology in the same way that craftwork and dialogue practice do. They activate a part of our nervous system that softens our boundaries and opens us to the possibility of metamorphosis and change. They do it in three ways.

First, imaginal cells act as emissaries of the heart, setting a pattern in motion for the expansion of awareness and the expression of beauty and freedom in a whole new form.

Second, they are resilient. When they first appear, because they are so different from the other cells the caterpillar's immune system attacks them. Yet they are able to withstand these attacks and continue to grow and expand.

Third, they are resonant and collaborative. As they are opposed, they form into small clumps that group together and lead to the transformation of the whole.

The potential of the imaginal cells lies dormant in the caterpillar most of the time. It may also lie dormant within us and within communities. What may trigger them is the same kind of stimulus that signals their development in the caterpillar: that with the anticipation of a transformational change there is a corresponding shift toward a greater transparency and softening of our boundaries, a blending of our surfaces that enables new, more resilient, collaborative, resonant heart-centred forms to take shape. These are enabled through different forms of collective engagement that are experienced as safe, natural, organic, respectful — almost routine — and eloquent in their simplicity.

In this context there is a turning and in the turning, place happens. New liberating structures evolve out of the old. Each is enabled to do its work through the presence of the other and in the turning, a butterfly is born.

EPILOGUE

A Wondrous Wildness:
Coming Home to a Place-based World

*"There is never the sense of having 'arrived' once and for
all… each moment must be met as new, as a wondrous
wildness to which one seeks to relate, not to control."*

– Sussman, 1995

The sense of arrival is never complete. We create places where we
find them. They appear as moments out of time, promises to be kept
— promises that are in keeping with a universe that is friendly to life
and our ongoing growth and evolution.

Several years ago I was invited to perform in a chapel in Lebanon
Penitentiary, a maximum-security prison near Toledo, Ohio.

"There is no need for concern," the event organizers said. "All the
men will appreciate your visit."

I didn't notice many expressions of appreciation amongst the 80
men as they seated themselves in the hot, dry chapel following lunch
that afternoon. I thought that Johnny Cash would be far more
suited to this event than I.

Soon after I started playing, a stocky man with tattoos down both arms stood up… walked slowly down the aisle… and out the door. How many will follow his lead, I wondered — they are not required to stay. My heart was racing. Distracted now, I was waiting for a second and perhaps a third to leave as well.

Shortly after, I heard the chapel door creak open as the man returned. He walked slowly up the centre aisle to the piano and stood beside it for a moment. Then he set a cold glass of water on the piano ledge, waited a moment longer, and then returned to his seat.

Everything changed in that moment. The simple act of seeing the condensation on the side of the glass was humbling. All the assumptions that had darkened my thoughts immediately dissolved. This was a touchstone moment. I realized that this was not a performance and that creating music involved more than simply getting the notes right. In order to connect with this group of men, I needed to connect with myself and *feel the room* first. As I brought more of myself into the room, including my vulnerability and unease, the men gave more of themselves back to me. The chapel in that moment took on a more intimate and human face.

When I shared this story with a colleague, his immediate response was to comment on the courage that is conveyed in this story. I said yes, the prison environment was completely alien and the hardened men… but before I could go further, he stopped me. "Yes, this took great courage on your part, but I was also thinking of that man — what courage did it take for him to step forward with this gesture of openness and hospitality in a room that seemed so unwelcoming of spontaneous expression."

The extending of the hand, the offering of the glass of water, the authenticity of that one gesture, was a precise articulation of what the moment called for. This brings to light another aspect of our relationship with place: as we turn toward the flow of life in all its beauty and possibility, we also touch moments of transcendence and humanness, a wondrous wildness, that acknowledges our participation in a place-based world.

Place happens. It is a natural and spontaneous act of the imagination that says to the world, "I am here." And when we do so, place offers itself to our imagination in a multitude of ways:

- Place happens when we respect the interdependence of the world — that plants, animals, people, groups and organizational systems all hold within them the inherent impulse to evolve toward becoming more and more of what they are essentially meant to be.

- Place happens when we accept the invitation to embrace the ecstatic spirit of Carnival through music, story, dance, poetry and song.

- Place happens when we welcome the stranger into our home, including the ember of desire burning with a quiet intensity in our own heart that is a stranger to ourselves.

- Place happens when we risk the expression of our prophetic voice — the voice whose words begin not from memory and fixed ideas but rather, as Robert Frost said, "as a lump in the throat and form on the tongue as we speak."

- Place happens when we see our gifts and aliveness — the discipline and practice of our craft — as the bond that creates a common ground of fellowship.

- Place happens when we embrace the ambiguity of the mythic landscape and with this the beautiful questions that draw us deeper into the mystery of life rather than to the answer.

- Place happens when we work with materials at hand that combine vision, imagination and craft to create outcomes that beautify our world and edify the human spirit.

- Place happens when we realize that we do not enter the world; we grow out of it. We hold the seed of our unfolding future within ourselves. Art comes from the prophetic soul that bristles in the soil beneath our feet.

- Place happens when there is an awakening to the life of a sacred economy — one enlivened through celebrating narratives, gifts and possibilities rather than correcting deficiencies, problems and needs.

- Place happens when we nourish the sanctuary that offers stillness, solitude and contemplation — the field of hidden wholeness that lies behind all things.

- Place happens when we live at the edges of all our plans. The artist is the outlier who mediates at the threshold of the visible and invisible worlds. The artist's work is to listen for the deeper music in the space between the notes.

- Place happens when we acknowledge the suffering in our loneliness by choosing to act from the space between. We are all artists when we stand at the threshold of imaginative sight and see what no one else is seeing.

- Place happens when we shift from the world of abstraction to being the placeholder for a more elemental feeling-centred life.

- Place happens through life's grace. "Easily, easily," composer Frederic Chopin would often say. "Do not force the notes." Learn instead to be apprentices to the art of touch so that you may hold the places in our world with a velvet touch.

- Place happens in each moment we can say Yes to the deep song that is alive in us now and yearns to reach out to embrace a larger world.

In the beginning we came into the world trailing clouds of glory and singing our own deep song. But all too soon our dream fades and the song dims. "Why do they shut me out of heaven?" poet Emily Dickinson asks. "Did I sing too loud?"

When the fundamental regenerative forces within our organization, community and ourselves are not flourishing and the call to a larger life is unheeded, we may feel shut out and alone in a placeless world, a world of absolutes in which we are not permitted to sing too loud. The dominant world of logos is still suspicious of the spontaneous nature of the feeling life and a place-based world. And yet from all we have explored here, it is clear the world longs to be enchanted again.

To be alive to place is to be alive to the love that binds our world, and our lives, together. This is the gift of place. In the turning to one another, we discover what it means to occupy our natural place in the world. It is our own way of looking at things. When we allow place to live through us in our relationships with nature, art and community, we become the love that brings and holds the world together.

Whatever its risks, heaven cannot find us if we are content to sing anything less than our own deep song. When we take up our ground and offer our own song of praise we also take up the timeless call to bring the world of place alive again.

PLACE-BASED LEADERSHIP AND THE SOUL OF PLACEMAKING:

AN INVITATION

Communities thrive when they host quality conversations, not because they have new building and conference centers.

– Edward Glaeser

To fulfill their search for ways to become more whole and more alive, leaders need to be asking, "How do I find the deeper current of my own identity — and how do we make society work better and evolve our cultural identity — through practices of place and placemaking?" Through sharing stories, to convey the message, and music, to deepen it, I and my colleagues have been creating generative spaces in leadership conferences and seminars and in communities and organizations for leaders to discover their own path toward creating cultures that nurture the soul of place and placemaking.

Specifically, we have been asking:

- What are the underpinnings that make up the soul of a place? In what ways do we nurture our own soul? And how does nurturing the soul of place empower our organizations, our communities and our own lives? What is the connection between our ability to thrive and our relationship to the soul of place itself?

- What is the emerging role of the leader in crafting places where life can thrive? What knowledge and perspectives do we need? What skills and resources? Which roles do we play, and which ones do we need to let go of and leave behind?

To learn more about *The Soul of Placemaking,* write to Michael through his website:

www.thesoulofplace.com

ACKNOWLEDGEMENTS

Just as a village raises a child, a community writes a book. A special expression of gratitude to all those colleagues and communities of practice who have inspired the writing of The Soul of Place:

Deb Higgins and The Fetzer Institute for convening the multi-year Leading for Transformation Dialogues and for supporting The Soul of Place project; Carol Pearson, Judy Brown and the partnership between The Fetzer Institute and The James MacGregor Burns Academy of Leadership; Cynthia Cherrey, Shelly Wilsey and The International Leadership Association; Sheryl Erickson for her vision and commitment in creating the Powers of Place Initiative and supporting our first forum at the Banff Centre; Nick Nissley, Katrina Donald, Colin Funk and other colleagues with Leadership Development at the Banff Centre for hosting, and Renee Levi, for co-convening, our first forum on the Powers of Place; Helga Breuninger, Volker Hann and The Breuninger Foundation for their generosity and continued support for the Soul of Place gatherings on Wasan Island in Muskoka; Julie Auger for her comprehensive documentation of our Banff forum and co-convening our first Wasan Island gathering; Bill Isaacs, Skip Griffin and Dialogos, where we are creating places of the heart and dialogues for regenerating the soul of the city; Paul Born, Sylvia Cheuy, Liz Weaver, Mark Cabaj and the community at Tamarack and The Collaborating Communities Institute for offering a platform to share and deepen my perspectives on the soul of place; Charles Holmes, Ann and Gary Ralston Stephanie Sauve, Avril Orloff and The Connecting for Change Community, where we have been creating large-group transformative conversations; Robert Lengel, Gary Larsen and the Academy of Leadership and Transformation, University of Texas, San Antonio where we frame executive leadership education around the integration of arts, sciences and humanities as the foundation for restoring a front porch culture and the health of the commons; Gayle Dempsey, Gary Froude and Muskoka Chautauqua for co-creating an inspired curriculum on place and placemaking through art, poetry, story and ceramics in regional schools; Orillia Mayor Angelo Orsi, co-chair Daphne Mainprize and the Mariposa Community Roundtable for envisioning the power of myth in re-imagining our story of place and community; Bob Stilger, Meg Wheatley, Susan Szpakowski, Marianne Knuth and many other colleagues at The Shambhala Institute for Authentic Leadership; Amy Lenzo, Juanita Brown, David Isaacs and the World Café Community; Victoria Cliché, David Horth and The Creative Education Foundation; Pamela Wilhelms and the Yosemite Leadership Academy and communities forming around the soul of the new economy; Peter Senge and The Society for Organizational Learning and Innovation Groups; Transforming Local Government.

And my teachers: Aldo Leopold, being native to this place; Christopher Alexander, the quality with no name; Emily Conrad, continuum and the life of the cells; Michelle Holliday, creating spaces for life; Sunshine Chen, the architecture of wonder; Bill Reed, regenerativity and conscious evolution; Peter Block, the structure of belonging; and Mark Nepo, who has taught me 7,000 ways to listen.

And, most importantly, my wife, Judy, and my mother, Laura, who both offered a steady hand, and Chopin, who transformed my world through his fingers — to each, a heartfelt "Thank you."

REFERENCES

Alexander, Christopher, and Hans Joachim Neiss and Maggie M. Moore. 2012. *Battle for the Life and Beauty of the Earth: A Struggle Between Two World-Systems.* The Center for Environmental Structure Series, New York: Oxford University Press.

Alexander, Christopher. 2002. *The Nature of Order, Book One: The Phenomena of Life.* Berkeley: The Center for Environmental Structure.

Bakewell, Sarah. 2011. *How to Live: A Life of Montaigne in One Question and Twenty Three Attempts At an Answer.* New York: Other Press.

Basso, Keith. 1996. *Wisdom Sits in Places: Landscape and Language among the Western Apache.* Albuquerque: University of New Mexico Press.

Berry, Wendell. 1981. *Recollected Essays 1965 to 1980.* New York: North Point Press.

Bird, Alan. 1991. *The Master in the Stone: An Interview with Alan Bird.* New York: *Parabola*, CRAFT, Volume XVI, Number 3, August.

Block, Peter. 2009. *Community: The Structure of Belonging.* San Francisco: Barrett-Koehler.

Bloomer, Kent C., and Charles W. Moore. 1977. *Body, Memory and Architecture*. New Haven, CT: Yale University Press.

Bly, Robert. 1983. *Times Alone: Selected Poems of Antonio Machado Wesleyan Poetry in Translation*. Middletown, CT: Wesleyan University Press.

Boethius, Ancius, and Victor Watts. 1999. *The Consolation of Philosophy*. New York: Penguin.

Bolier, David. *Think Like a Commoner: A Short Introduction to the Life of the Commons*. 2014. Gabriola Island, BC: New Society Publishers.

Brooks, David. 2010. *The Summoned Life*. New York: *New York Times*.

Brown, Ian. "Should we set half aside for nature?" Toronto: *The Globe and Mail*, October 2013.

Brueggemann, Walter. 2010. *Journey to the Common Good*. Louisville, KY: Westminster John Knox Press.

Brueggemann, Walter. 2001. *The Prophetic Imagination*, second edition. Minneapolis: Fortress Press.

Carver, Raymond. 2000. *All of Us: The Collected Poems*. New York: Vintage.

Cary, John, and Courtney E. Martin. 2012. *Dignifying Design*. New York: *The New York Times*, October 6.

Carter, Paul. 2009. *Dark Writing: Geography, Performance, Design*. Honolulu: University of Hawaii Press.

Cather, Willa. 2010. *(The Original) Death Comes for the Archbishop 1927*. Amazon Digital Services.

Creates, Marlene. 1997. *Places of Presence: Newfoundland kin and ancestral land, Newfoundland 1989–1991*. St John's, NF: Killick Press.

Damasio, Antonio. 2005. *Descartes' Error and the Future of Human Life*. New York: *Scientific American*, October 144–149.

Dooling, D. M. 1985. *A Way of Working: The Spiritual Dimension of Craft*. New York: *Parabola*, November.

Dreyfus, Herbert, and Sean Dorrance Kelly. 2011. *All Things Shining: Reading the Western Classics to Find Meaning in a Secular Age*. Washington DC: Free Press.

Egan, Timothy. 2005. *The Worst Hard Time: The Untold Story of Those Who Survived the Dust Bowl*. Boston: Houghton Mifflin.

Eigeldinger, Jean-Jacques. 1987. *Chopin: Pianist and Teacher*. Cambridge, UK: Cambridge University Press.

Fritz, Robert. 1989. *The Path of Least Resistance, How to Become the Creative Force in Your Life*. New York: Ballantine.

Gallagher, Beth. 2007. *Profiles From the Past, Faces of the Future, Waterloo 150*. Waterloo, ON: City of Waterloo.

Glaeser, Edward. 2012. *Triumph of the City: How Our Greatest Invention Makes Us Richer, Smarter, Greener, Healthier, and Happier* (Penguin Reprint edition). New York: Penguin.

Havel, Vaclav. 1992. *Summer Meditations*. New York: Knopf.

Hawken, Paul. 1993. *The Ecology of Commerce*. New York: Harper Collins.

Huddle, Norrie. 1997. *Butterfly*. New York: Huddle Books.

Isaacson, Walter. 2011. *Steve Jobs*. New York: Simon and Schuster.

Johnson, Robert A. 1991. *Transformation: Understanding the Three Levels of Masculine Consciousness*. San Francisco: Harper San Francisco.

Jones, Michael. 2006. *Leading Artfully: Awakening the Commons of the Imagination*. Bloomington, IN: Trafford Publishing.

Keillor, Garrison. 2011. *Good Poems, American Places*. New York: Penguin.

Kenyon, Jane, and Bill Moyers. 1995. *The Language of Life: A Festival of Poets*. New York: Doubleday.

Kimmelman, Michael. 2011. *Tahrir to Zuccotti: The Power of Place; Protesters and Cities Find Unity by Sharing Common Ground*. Toronto: *New York Times* supplement in the *Toronto Star*.

Lawrence, D. H. 1993. In *Searching Out the Headwaters* (Sarah Bates, et al). Washington: Island Press.

Leopold, Aldo. 1999. *The Essential Aldo Leopold Quotations and Commentaries* edited by Curt Meine and Richard L. Knight. Madison, WI: University of Wisconsin Press.

Lopez, Barry. 2001. *Arctic Dreams*. New York: Vintage.

Lorca, Frederico G. 1955. *In Search of Duende*, edited and translated by Christopher Maurer. London: New Directions.

Lyle, John T. 1994. *Regenerative Design for Sustainable Development*. New York: John Wiley and Sons.

MacFarlane, Robert. 2012. *The Old Ways, A Journey on Foot*. New York: Viking.

MacFarquar, Neil. 2012. *Amid Syria's Uprising Creativity Flourishes*. New York: *The New York Times*, January 1.

Martin, Roger. 2011. *Canada, Like Steve Jobs, Should Zero In on Innovation.* Toronto: Globe and Mail, November.

McKay, Don. 2011. *The Shell of the Tortoise.* Kentville, NS: Gaspereau Press.

Meadows, Donella. 1997. *Places to Intervene in a System.* San Francisco: Whole Earth News.

Michaels, Anne. 2010. *Winter's Vault.* New York: Vintage.

Mills, Kenneth G. 2008. *The Candy Man's Son: Memoir of Kenneth G. Mills.* Toronto: Kenneth G. Mills Foundation.

McGinn, D. 2013. *"Meet Brent Comber The 'Wood Whisperer."* Toronto: *The Globe and Mail.*

Mockbee, Samuel. 1998. "The Rural Studio" in *The Everyday and Architecture.* Hoboken, NJ: John Wiley and Sons.

Mount, Nick. 2013. *"Sunshine Sketches of a Small Town* Reviewed." Toronto: *The Globe and Mail.*

Moyers, Bill. 1995. *The Language of Life: A Festival of Poets.* New York: Doubleday.

Muir, John. 1997. *Nature Writings.* New York: Penguin.

Muller, Wayne. 1999. *Sabbath: Restoring the Sacred Rhythm of Rest.* New York: Bantam.

Needleman, Carla. 1993. *The Work of Craft: An Inquiry into the Nature of Craft and Craftsmanship.* New York: Kodansha International.

O'Donohue, John. 2005. *Beauty: The Invisible Embrace.* New York: Harper Perennial.

Oldenburg, Ray. 2002. *Celebrating the Third Place: Inspiring Stories about the "Great Good Places" at the Heart of Our Communities.* Cambridge, MA: De Capo.

Oldenburg, Ray. 2000. *Celebrating the Third Place: Inspiring Stories About the " Great Good Places" At the Heart of Our Communities.* New York: Marlowe and Co.

Olson, Charles. 1997. *The Collected Poems of Charles Olson Excluding Maximus Poems.* Berkeley: University of California Press.

Orr, David W. 2002. *The Nature of Design, Ecology, Culture, and Human Intention.* Oxford, UK: Oxford University Press.

Otto, Walter F. 1965. *Dionysus, Myth and Cult* translated and with an introduction by Robert F. Palmer. Bloomington, IN: Indiana University Press.

Parini, Jay. 1999. *Robert Frost: A Life.* New York: Owl Books Henry Holt and Co.

Paulnack, Karl. 2009. *Welcome Address To the Boston Conservatory Freshman Class 2004.* The Boston Conservatory: http://www.bostonconservatory.edu/music/karl-paulnack-welcome-address.

Pitts, Gordon. 2013. *Rebuilding Capitalism From the Basics.* Toronto: *Globe and Mail,* March.

Purdy, Al, and Margaret Atwood and Sam Solecki. 2000. *Beyond Remembering: The Collected Works of Al Purdy.* Madeira Park, BC: Harbour Press.

Raz, Guy. 2011. *Keith Jarrett: Alone in Rio and Ready to Fail.* All Things Considered, NPR, November 14.

Reed, Bill. 2006. *"Shifting Our Mental Model — 'Sustainability' to Regeneration."* Boston: Rethinking Sustainable Construction Conference, September.

Rowe, Jonathon. "The Hidden Commons 2001." Bainbridge Island: Yes Magazine and Positive Futures Network.

Russell, Jean M. 2013. *Thrivability: Breaking Through To A World That Works*. Devon, UK: Triarchy Press.

Roskill, Mark. 1997. *The Letters of Vincent Van Gogh*. New York: Touchstone.

Sachs, Oliver. 2007. *Musicophilia: Tales of Music and the Brain*. New York: Knopf.

Savage, Candace. 2012. *The Geography of Blood: Unearthing Memory From a Prairie Landscape*. Toronto: Greystone.

Sennett, Richard. 2009. *The Craftsman*. New Haven, CN: Yale University Press.

Sinclair, Cameron, and Kate Stohr (eds.). 2006. *Design Like You Give a Damn*. New York: Metropolis Books.

Sioui, Georges E. 1999. *Huron Wendat: The Heritage of the Circle*. Vancouver: UBC Press.

Snyder, Gary. 1990. *Practice of the Wild*. New York: North Point Press.

Stafford, Kim. 2003. *The Muses Among Us: Eloquent Listening and Other Pleasures of the Writer's Craft*. Athens, GA: University of Georgia Press.

Stafford, William E. 1999. *The Way It Is*. St. Paul, MN: Graywolf.

Sussman, Linda. 1995. *Speech of the Grail: A Journey Through Speaking That Heals and Transforms*. Hudson, NY: Lindisfarne.

Swimme, Brian T., and Mary Evelyn Tucker. 2011. *Journey of the Universe*. New Haven, CN: Yale University Press.

Szpakowski, Susan. 2010. *The Little Book of Practice for Authentic Leadership in Action*. Halifax, NS: ALIA.

Tapscott, Don. 2012. *Four Principles for An Open World*. TED Global, June.

Thompson, Patricia. 2011. "*The Dark Horse Conversation: Nonprofit Leaders Talk about Vocational, Organizational and Civic Renewal.*" Toronto: Metcalf Foundation.

Van der Ryn, Sim, and Stuart Cohen. 2007. *Ecological Design, 10th Anniversary Edition*. Washington DC: Island Press.

Van Gelder, Sarah, and YES! Magazine. 2011. "This Changes Everything: Occupy Wall Street and the 99% Movement." San Francisco: Berrett-Koehler.

Wagoner, David. 1979. *Collected Poems 1956 to 76* (4th edition). Bloomington, IN: University of Indiana.

Walker, Alan, and Jessica Duchen and Jeremy Siepmann. 2010. "*Chopin: His Life, His Genius, His Legacy.*" Bristol: BBC Music Magazine, February.

Walter, E. V. 1988. *Placeways, A Theory of the Human Environment*. Chapel Hill, NC: University of North Carolina Press.

Weiner, Eric. 2012. "*Where Heaven and Earth Come Closer.*" New York: *The New York Times*, March 9.

Wheatley, Margaret J. 2002. *Turning to One Another; Simple Conversations to Restore Hope in the Future*. San Francisco: Barrett Koehler.

ENDNOTES

1. I first heard the story of "the Land in the Middle" from Sherry Lawson's brother, Mark Douglas Biidaanakwad (Cloud Approaching), who is one of the keepers of the fish fence.

2. I studied for several years in Toronto with Kenneth G. Mills who, through his piano teaching and conversations, offered instruction in how the beauty of place serves as a touchstone we can create within ourselves.

3. This description of their land was articulated in part through stories from their small-group conversations. I also adapted the description from *The Little Book of Practice in Authentic Leadership*, a beautiful book on leadership practice written by Susan Szpakowski (2009), the founding director of ALIA, the Halifax-based Authentic Leadership, who also attended the conference.

4. Some of this history can be found in Beth Gallagher's *Profiles From the Past, Faces of the Future, Waterloo 150*, published by the City of Waterloo.

5. From a conversation with Sunshine Chen, a graduate of the architectural co-op program at the University of Waterloo. Sunshine is part of the social innovation initiative in Waterloo and works with media-based story building to create place-

based communities.

6. With notes from my colleague Judy Brown, with whom I wrote an introduction to the book, *The Transforming Leader;* editor Carol Pearson, Berrett-Koehler publishers, 2012.

7. From the invitation letter to employees from Jaya Kumar, former president and CEO of Quaker Foods. I was a consultant and reflection partner on the design team with lead project consultant Charles Holmes, singer-songwriter Barbara Mcafee, graphic artist Avril Orloff and curators Gary and Ann Ralston. We were invited to design and facilitate several large employee and stakeholder engagement meetings for Quaker Foods and the PepsiCo Global Nutrition Group. The framework was originally conceived for the Dalai Lama Peace Summit and the Connecting for Change Conversations supported in part by the Fetzer Institute in September 2009.

8. With notes from a dialogue and artistry forum in February 2010 with Peter Block and his reflections from conversations with Old Testament theologian Walter Brueggemann.

9. From William Stafford's poem "When I Met My Muse."

10. Adapted from Doug Forrester's "Prairie Grasses," unpublished, written for the Citizen's Campaign.

11. With notes from an article in the *Toronto Star* by columnist Rick Salutin, "Spanish Protesters Go Back to the Roots of Democracy with Assemblies," July 20, 2012.

THE SOUL OF PLACE:

GLOSSARY

We cannot enter the future without first knowing its language. And our future will become known to us primarily through a language that is place-based.

THE PURPOSE OF PLACE

As we enter the world of leadership, being place-based is how we keep the dream of childhood alive, and with this dream, the source of our own creative power and well-being.

Being place-based also respects the appetite many have to engage our world through something more than the anonymous transactional relationships that make up much of our public lives. When we feel connected to a place our relationships are more meaningful and significant and we tend to the places in our world in a more caring way.

Experiencing the soul of a place also reminds us that we are 'creatures of belonging.' As such, places help us feel more rooted, more at home and more connected to something larger than ourselves.

Raising the consciousness of place also increases our awareness of the extent to which we are shaped by our surroundings including nature, culture and community as much as we shape them. That is, we learn to appreciate how each evokes something from the other and that we are essentially sentient beings whose moods and emotions are deeply influenced by the subtle forces of tonality and atmosphere that move around and about us.

So, the purpose of place is to inspire a new guiding narrative, one rooted in a shift in our world view from seeing our environment as a backdrop primarily constructed out of impersonal bits and pieces of things, a legacy from the industrial age, to a world that is alive, complex, artful and intelligent — a world of place.

A GLOSSARY

To explore this emerging narrative there are several recurring concepts that I would like to explore. This glossary represents the underpinnings from which many place-based innovations and initiatives may evolve.

SANCTUARY

Place is a sanctuary where we feel most at home and most naturally ourselves. It is also a crucible for transformation and change.

Place can be a physical location, time in nature, a form of craft, a calling, an idea, a meeting or a community. It is a feeling and a possibility; it offers a sense of welcome, of invitation and inclusivity.

As sanctuary, place is where we go for solace and rest. Without rest there can be no regeneration. Place may also serve as a crucible for transformation and change. Many can share stories of how a place offered a crucible moment that was life-changing. In this context, places can be complex and multi-faceted. As a sanctuary, if there is too much security, there is no growth. As a crucible, if there is too much change, there is no rest. It is in the middle of these two poles that the soul learns.

REGENERATION

To be regenerative means giving more back to the world than we consume from the world.

Places are dynamic, complex and self-evolving. As such they thrive by building upon and regenerating themselves from the inside out. We have learned to think things apart. Now we need to think things together again. It means shifting our focus from sustainability based on a model of scarcity to one of generosity based on how we integrate the parts so places can continuously regenerate and renew themselves. To regenerate and thrive relies on our abilities for service and stewardship. To be regenerative does not imply that the world is limitless — there exist certain natural limits to growth that we need to preserve — but these limits we impose tend to be man-made not nature-based. We need new stories that remind us we live in an ever-expanding and generative universe in which, when we create a space for life to happen, opportunities are replenished, not diminished, by the creative demands we place upon them.

ECOLOGY

To see ourselves as part of an ecosystem is not a question of surviv-ability but of suitability. How do I belong here? How can I co-exist with others? What is my element and what am I most fitted for?

Seeing the world as not divided but diverse and interdependent is based on the realization that we do not sit above the rest of life but are instead intimately embedded in life and in nature. We recognize that we need to change our assumptions regarding how we see the world. The notion that we exist in an industrial age with its silos and hierarchies where the outside world was assumed to be fixed, static and inert is changing. We are now entering the age of biology — an age when we have the opportunity to discover how to grow to become fully ourselves and also interdependent with the larger whole. A beautiful image describing how we find our own element is found in German poet Rainer Maria Rilke's image of the swan. Awkward and lumbering on land, it releases itself to the water, where it finds itself in its own element, serene and sure as it glides with regal composure farther and farther on. In this instance the swan becomes part of a larger ecology that welcomes it home.

SONG

Music brings us home to feeling, to the heart and to the mystery of life. Music renders the invisible visible and transports us back in time.

The song that created the world lives in us still. Underlying our words is a rhythm and cadence that carries the line just as the craft-worker's ears are attuned and guided by the sound of the tools. All great music is inspired by the natural sounds of the world. We return to places because they carry a tone, an atmosphere that appeals to us in a particular way. Each is a unique articulation of universal tones, timbres, rhythms, harmonics and sororities… the entire earth functions like a musical score.

Sounds that arise spontaneously transpose the random and chaotic energies within and around us into an ordered dance and a more coherent state. As such, the deep song we hear in the wind, the water, the words, and tools all remind us that sound is as much a part of our biological inheritance as any other physical function. It ensures our survival and fires our creativity. Nature sings for its own pleasure. To create sounds together as a celebration of place is an expression of our own joy.

DESTINY

Destiny puts us in a conversation with a far horizon and a larger unknown and teaches us how to hold the ground on which we are standing at the same time.

Conversations regarding our sense of place in the future shift our focus from short-term planning and goal-setting to the far horizon and a different relationship with place and with time. Destiny conversations give us more space to consider new possibilities. For example, questions rooted in our aspirations for the future give us hope and time to dream, questions rooted on what we know from our heritage and history give us context and certainty, and questions rooted in what is known in the present offer a sense of security and continuity. Leaders will need to hold a perspective on all three places — future, past and present — at the same time in order to navigate in times of unpredictability and sudden change. Envisioning our destiny and a larger unknown sets us on a pilgrimage, a path poet Antonio Machado says "can only be laid by walking," where reading the landscape of place rather than focusing on pre-established goals will serve as our primary guide.

MYTH

Myth is found in the wholeness behind all things. An enduring myth will give meaning to a place for hundreds of years.

When we weave a story, particularly a mythic or spiritual story, around a place, we rediscover the core values we want to live by. This may serve as our creation myth, and this myth may serve as a portal into our inner life together. Leaders who shape the culture of a place through the circulation of these larger-than-life stories help to contextualize the future they want to create for themselves. To re-inhabit the places we are in, we need to recreate a new guiding mythic story that describes it. These stories serve as the most powerful building block for creating a regenerative culture for the future. Like music and the arts, myths are an intimate part of our biology. We carry their memory in our cells; they form a part of our common inheritance. As such, there is much in the mythic world of ancestors, destiny, history, pilgrimage, story and enchantment that is alive in us still, even if it cannot be explained in full.

SOUL

Where spirit seeks unity, peace and harmony that shapes our personality, the soul is found in the undergrowth, in our vulnerability and the depths of experience. Soul shapes our character.

The soul is the mystery and the inexplicable in human life. It connects our day-to-day experience with a sense of depth, of destiny and productive ambiguity. The soul is the opaque light, the roots, the soil and the undergrowth. We also associate the work of the soul with life's possibilities including what we imagine when we create time for reflection, for dreaming, imagining and fantasizing. This is often when the soul assumes its other role as the disrupter pushing us to let go of old forms and conventional ways of seeing in order to think and imagine life anew. To engage the soul is to also be in empathic resonance with the world. That is, to recognize that to know another is also to be known by the other — an act of mutual reciprocity — which draws out our own vulnerability and directs it toward the care and concern for the well-being of the soul of the world.

BEAUTY

If there is to be a soul of a new economy it will be based not only on power and influence, but on beauty.

The ugliness of our world is found in the sameness of things. Too often we engineer a utilitarian world that has no room for beauty or soul. What if our buildings told stories and our public spaces were spacious, warm and inviting dwelling spaces where people who may be strangers to one another would want to gather? To engage the soul of a place is to return the world to beauty. And when we engage the beauty of the world, we not only inspire; we also craft and innovate and implement new possibilities.

Yet in matters of beauty we must 'tell it slant.' Beauty dazzles and will blind us if we look full on. So beauty is often found at the margins, along the thresholds and at the edge of things. It dwells just out of reach, just beyond words and on the periphery of our vision. It is this sense of the depth and presence of beauty, the awareness that we cannot stop and capture it, that enriches the soul. During a recent conference we noted several ways that beauty was key to its success… We introduced beauty through live improvised music — music that was created as an invitation rather than a performance. We introduced beauty through sitting and moving in silence and through sharing individual stories and small-group conversations. And we wandered outdoors to find objects of beauty and bring them back to assemble together as symbols for what the meaning of the day had been for everyone. In this way beauty served as the mirror that reflected the beauty of our own spirit back to us.

EMERGENCE

Creating places where life can thrive will serve as one of the great animating stories for our future.

To imagine places in the future that are vibrant, alive and nature-based we will need language to describe them. It will be a language, for example, that sees place in the context of organic networks rather than formal structures. We will look for signs of agility, adaptivity, flexibility, permeability, emergence, openness and diversity. Our ways of knowing our world will shift from concepts and plans to pathways and pilgrimages and, with this, our ways of navigating will become more subtle and tactile, our boundaries more porous and open to influence and our awareness of the quality of places and spaces in our environment more discerning. As such the biological age will be one in which we will focus more on informal gatherings and the movement of emergent, spontaneous collective action rather than formal strategies. As our capacities and pace for learning quickens, our sense of place will become more refined and deeply felt. We will be more aware of the human cost of the loss of place on our own collective and systemic capacities for growth and integration as well as our psychic sense of safety, protection and well-being.

EMBODIMENT

All life is movement. And in this movement whatever we see, we become.

We often don't think of bodily knowing and cellular movement as a form of intelligence that holds equal standing with the intellect. When we do think of the body we relate to it in ways that are primarily muscular and skeletal. We associate the body with images of rigidity and resistance and the interaction between sinews, nerves, bones, density and structure. But the much larger part of the body is made up of water molecules and connective tissue. This alternate body is cellular rather than muscular and it moves in space through a blending of fluid motion rather than the force of effort. With this fluid body whatever we see in a place, we become. We don't observe; we inhabit the wind, the trees and the waters. Understanding this alternate aspect of body structure is helpful in thinking about place and placemaking. The muscular body, which is more individually oriented and transactional, moves through space with greater force of effort than the cellular or fluid body, which blends in intimate resonance with its surroundings.

So as a pianist moving in this fluid body when I play I am also being played. My fingers blend with the tactile sensation of the piano keys and follow the lead of this cellular intelligence that guides my hands as I play.

CRAFT

Craft opens a path to bodily knowing and the body, more than the intellect, takes in the fullness of whatever place we are in.

Finding one's craft opens up a powerful relationship with place and with a larger unknown. This may be because, through our craft, we see place as the home that nourishes our gifts so that they may be enacted in the service of a larger goal. Through the arc of time there have been two paths: *Homo sapiens*, man the thinker and *Homo faber*, man the maker. With *Homo sapiens* we establish our competence in the world. With *Homo faber* we establish our craft. Both are important but too often we have allowed our competence to dominate and our craft suffers from neglect. When our craft suffers, our connection to the soul of place suffers as well. Each is closely interconnected with the other. The resurgence of craft leads to work that is more holistic and integrative. We can practice our craft in any field. To be 'hands on' simply involves doing our best and seeing our craft as our 'art form' in whatever field we choose. The resurgence of craft involves getting at the root of things through using local materials and local wisdom drawn from the place itself. This resurgence is leading to an attitude to work that is wholehearted and integrates the mind with the heart and the hand.

The Third Place

It is the third place through which the soul speaks.

In a group it may be through story, music, art, poetry or silence. The third thing breaks a pattern and opens the way for something new and unexpected to occur. It gives a place its soul. In community the third thing may be the commons, the public square, the neglected back lot or the space in between. The third is found in the overlap where we discover what we hold most in common. It was always the function of the third space to magnify the hidden dimensions of the other so that no person remained fully invisible to the whole. Everyone was seen. The third place also ensures the health of our common-pool resources of air, water and soil — all of which we rely upon together.